© Henry Rack 1969

First published in 1969
by Epworth Press

Printed and bound by
The Garden City Press Limited
Letchworth, Hertfordshire

SBN 7162 0078 3

23147/2⅛8

The New Reformation Series

THE past few years have seen a theological ferment which some think could herald a new Reformation. Whether it will do so is impossible to tell; in any case it is dangerous to draw historical parallels.

Yet over the last two centuries there has been a new Renaissance, a cultural revolution, which dwarfs the old. And the danger is that, in all the excitement and our desire to do something, we may be influenced more by the fashions of the age than by fidelity to truth. Christians may be tempted to count the advance of the Gospel in headlines rather than in men and women set free for living, and to substitute journalism and TV debate for the exploration of ultimate questions in the light of the new knowledge we have gained.

At the same time, theology must not be confined to the schools, and there is no more satisfactory feature of the present situation than the interchange between professionals and non-experts which paperback publishing has facilitated. After all, it is often the man or woman in the street, the office, the factory, or the laboratory who asks the questions. The attempts to answer must not be whispered in the polysyllables of common rooms or the jargon of seminars.

It is the aim of this series to dig deep into the foundations both of Christianity and of life, but to bring what is discovered to the surface in a form which can be seen clearly and understood by anyone who is sensitive to the problems of our time and is willing to exercise his mind on them and on the possibility that the Christian tradition has something relevant to say. The books will not be too lengthy and they will avoid footnotes, critical apparatus and too much technicality. The authors have been chosen because they are scholars and experts in the subjects assigned to them, but also because they are alive to the contemporary world and concerned about communication.

The method will be to look for truth about the nature of the universe and of human life and personality by seeking a fruitful and illuminating interplay between modern questions and insights and traditional Christian assertions and understandings. There is no intention to seek simply a restatement of Christianity in terms 'acceptable to modern man'. The Editors believe that it is as misguided to suggest that the truth of Christianity depends on what modern man can accept as it is simply to reiterate the ancient formulations of orthodoxy. The vital questions are 'How may we be led to see what is true?'; 'What is the nature of theological truth and how is it related to other kinds?'; 'What resources have we for understanding and meeting the real needs of men?'; 'How does Christianity look in the light of our answers to these questions and how does Christianity contribute to these answers?'

We hope that this series may be a modest contribution towards *aggiornamento* if not reformation.

General Editor: GORDON S. WAKEFIELD

Advisory Board

W. RUSSELL HINDMARSH
Professor of Atomic Physics, University of Newcastle upon Tyne

DAVID JENKINS
Fellow and Chaplain of the Queen's College, Oxford. Canon Theologian of Leicester

JOHN KENT
Lecturer in Ecclesiastical History and Doctrine, University of Bristol

DAVID PATON
Secretary of the Missionary and Ecumenical Council of the Church Assembly. Hon. Canon of Canterbury

COLIN WILLIAMS
Chicago Theological Seminary

iv

Contents

To
ELIZABETH BRODIE RACK

Preface

To FORESTALL misunderstanding (and perhaps even disappointment) two things need to be said about this book. First, it is not an attempt to create a scheme to rival or replace existing schemes of public and private devotion, fitted for men of the present century. Such an attempt would not merely be beyond my powers, it would also be (for reasons which the book should reveal) the wrong way forward from our contemporary problems of spirituality. Rather, as is explained in more detail in Chapter 1, this book is an attempt to put spirituality in a reasonable historical perspective and to suggest the origin and nature of some of the basic problems now facing any attempt at spirituality.

The second point to make clear is that an inquiry of the kind undertaken here must necessarily touch upon a great deal and a great variety of specialized subject-matter both inside and outside the narrowly religious field; indeed it is part of my purpose to show that it is impossible to treat 'spirituality' in isolation as a 'purely religious' problem. This creates obvious problems of expertise which I have certainly not overcome; it will become clear, for example, that I have drawn very freely on secondary materials where these provided convenient pointers to the problems I wished to illustrate, and that on such matters as psychology and sociology I am not even claiming to attempt to popularize the findings of the professionals. I am attempting, rather, to give a rough sketch map for explorers concerned with the subject of this book. Here, it is suggested, is the kind of territory which must be investigated; here, I think, are the obstacles which cannot be avoided. Even if the nature of the areas and the character of the obstacles are not exactly as they are described here, they still exist to be investigated and encountered and they cannot safely be ignored.

I would like to acknowledge the benefit received in numerous conversations on spirituality and other related subjects in the Manchester regional Renewal Group; and with my friends Douglas Brown, John Kent and David Pailin, who have taught me a great deal without being in any way responsible for the use I have made of what they have said, even where certain writings of theirs are noted as supplying some of my material.

HENRY RACK

November 1967

1. Introduction

1. The Question of Definition

To AVOID unnecessary confusion about the subject and scope of this book, it will be as well to define how the term 'spirituality' will be used. Normally the term is used in a sense derived from a distinction well established in the Roman Catholic Church, which has been described by, for example, Pourrat in his work on *Christian Spirituality*. Pourrat[1] distinguishes between Dogmatic, Moral and Spiritual Theology. 'Spiritual' Theology is based on dogmatic and moral theology but is 'above them' in being a theology dealing 'not with abstract statements of faith and objective laws of conduct, but with the life in Christ itself, the reality of that union with him, which all tradition in some form would assert as the meaning of our salvation'. For Pourrat this 'Spiritual Theology' is briefly described as 'that part of theology which deals with Christian perfection

I

and the ways that lead to it'. It includes the study of special mystical states for the few, which cannot be 'worked up to' by effort; and, more important, the study of 'ascetic' theology which concerns the exercises of aspirants on the 'ordinary' way to perfection: this, by the way, includes two essential elements – the renunciation of self, and a firm determination to follow or imitate Christ. Pourrat gives Luke 9:23 as the biblical foundation text for the whole design: 'If any man would come after me, let him deny himself and take up his cross daily and follow me.'

This is a clear and useful description but it is (particularly when Pourrat speaks of 'ascetic' theology) too restricted in scope, too closely tied to one kind of Christian tradition – which seems, moreover, to be assumed as the only possible tradition. One purpose of the present study is to be more comprehensive in scope, more willing to examine what is taken for granted in the Pourrat type of definition. I therefore propose to use the term 'spirituality' to cover a more general but also more fundamental inquiry into the whole Christian enterprise of pursuing, achieving and cultivating communion with God, which includes both public worship and private devotion, and the results of these in actual Christian life. The study will not be limited to the ideals of any one Christian tradition, and my concern is less (for example) with the detailed reform of worship than with the problems of how any kind of worship is possible today; less with the technique of saying one's prayers than with the conditions now affecting any attempt at prayer. It will be suggested that any attempt at particular types of spirituality today must be preceded by this kind of fundamental analysis and understanding, and that the failure to carry out this kind of inquiry is a basic weakness in much modern writing and practice in the field of spirituality as it has been broadly defined here.

2

2. The Need for Analysis

It may be as well to elaborate a little on this point. Although, as has been said, the scope of this study will not be limited to any one tradition and it will not be taken for granted that there *is* one basic tradition which alone can properly be termed 'spirituality', much of the material and argument will be concerned with the situation of Protestant Christianity in the West. Although this is taken to include various types of Anglicanism as well, and naturally involves comparisons and contrasts with Roman Catholic tradition, the limitations may be felt to be considerable. However, it may be claimed that any serious attempt to study any type of spirituality in depth and comparatively will raise most of the problems worth discussing about the subject as a whole. But the best justification for concentrating on Protestantism in the Western world lies in the nature of the inquiry undertaken here. For if the main concern is to analyse the conditions under which any attempt at spirituality now operates, then it is just here – in Protestantism in the West – that the conditions I have in mind most clearly and forcefully operate. It is Western urban civilization which increasingly affects the rest of the world, no matter how many qualifications one may add. (National and racial antagonisms to the West, after all, often amount to repaying the West in its own coin.) As to Protestantism, the point here is mainly that Protestantism, compared with other forms of Christianity, has historically shown itself peculiarly swift, sensitive and far-reaching in positive reactions to the secular development of the West. No judgement is made here about the goodness or badness of this tendency. For our present purpose, the development and problems of Western Protestant spirituality provide particularly useful materials

3

for making clear, more generally, the conditions and problems of spirituality today.

The condition of contemporary Protestant spirituality also illustrates very forcibly the need of analysis – and analysis of the fundamental kind which it is proposed to undertake here. First, Protestant piety (as distinct from piety in the 'Catholic' tradition – Roman and Anglican) has tended, for various reasons, to be suspicious of a conscious analysis and cultivation of spirituality. It will be claimed in due course that this is a weakness, not merely because in practice it has led to self-deception and lack of religious depth, but also because it may well reflect a wrong estimate of the nature of religion in human life. That is to say, it may exaggerate the common assumption that religion is instinctive in mankind, or at least can be unconsciously acquired, whereas in fact the opposite may really be the truth. Second, when Protestants are reluctantly converted to some attempt at a designed spirituality they are all the more open to ill-considered borrowing of techniques based on unexamined and possibly incompatible assumptions. For example, Churches which continue to centre their piety on preaching and Bible-reading may refurnish their chapels with central altars and side-pulpits while continuing a poorly attended quarterly Communion service. It is not in fact very easy or profitable to graft practices from one tradition on to another when the underlying religious and theological assumptions are different. All this points to the need to analyse our fundamental religious presuppositions, whatever they are, and also to examine how they compare with the present state of our religious consciousness, as well as the general consciousness of our time. This is far more important than a hasty grasping at 'solutions', for it may turn out that in the present state of Christianity we shall have to live with questions rather than answers, to emphasize reflection rather than action for its own sake: an unpopular but necessary counsel.

In such a situation one may perhaps be consoled by the words of Matthew Arnold who, in a not dissimilar situation, was accused of being impractical and of advocating 'a religion breathing a spirit of cultivated inaction, making its believer refuse to lend a hand at uprooting the definite evils on all sides of us, and filling him with antipathy against the reforms and reformers which try to extirpate them'; not to mention the conservatives who blame all critics, particularly critics who do not propose solutions. To all this Arnold's reply was: 'But what if rough and coarse action, ill-calculated action, action with insufficient light, is, and has for a long time been, our bane? What if our urgent want now is, not to act at any price, but rather to lay in a stock of light for our difficulties? . . . to make the primary need . . . to consist in enlightening ourselves and qualifying ourselves to act less at random, . . .'[2]

3. The Mode of Analysis

If the primary need in our contemporary religious problems (including those of spirituality) is for analysis, what mode of analysis is most profitable? It should be an analysis designed to reveal and assess assumptions and presuppositions which often lie unnoticed and unrealized behind particular schemes of spirituality. It is just here that the really fundamental questions about spirituality, with which this essay is mainly concerned, come in. The mode of analysis proposed here is as follows:

(1) Much religious discussion and action proceeds on the assumption that religion is a kind of instinct in all men. It may be conceded that today this is more often invisible than it used to be, but essentially (it seems to be assumed) it

5

is present in the very nature of man. In particular, the need and even the desire for worship must really be present in all, though only a minority in fact practise it explicitly. The problem for a modern spirituality is therefore to evoke this latent instinct by some congenially modern procedure: hence much talk and activity in terms of 'renewal'. The question ought to be raised whether the underlying assumption here is really valid. Perhaps religious belief and activity is acquired and learned, not instinctive. Perhaps in any case such capacity as we have, let alone the conditions for using it, may be so affected by the condition of society that the nature and very possibility of spirituality (and not merely its mode of expression) may now be affected.

(2) If there is any truth in this point of view, then some inquiry into the nature of the consciousness of contemporary men – how it has arisen and how this has affected religion – is perhaps the first inquiry of all to make; and obviously it will be a more fundamental inquiry than the common attempt of reformers to 'modernize' the presentation of traditional religious forms. One would be engaged, in fact, in an attempt to view the life of religion in its setting in the material and mental conditions of a developing world which affects any mode of spirituality at all. In this attempt one would have at least to be open to the possibility that what one is studying may reveal that real changes have taken place in the human psyche by 'secular' means, and that these changes affect the situation and even the nature of the religious experience, and so its possible expression in spirituality.

Such an inquiry might profitably follow two lines of analysis:

(a) The *internal* problems and pressures (material and mental) of religious groups: e.g. of the Christian Church as a whole, as distinct from secular society; or the peculiar difficulties faced by Protestants as distinct from Catholics; or the peculiar difficulties of particular types of Protestant.

(b) The *external* problems and pressures of the secular world at large, in which religious men and institutions also share: e.g. the effects of the social and intellectual development of the Western world, particularly in the last 150 years or so, on religious life.

One theme of the present essay is that both of these lines of analysis have to be taken seriously in any attempt at a realistic assessment of the state of modern Christianity and its spirituality. It will be argued that attempts at a modern spirituality often miss the mark and are unlikely to be effective because it has too readily been assumed that the human condition and its treatment are essentially changeless beneath only superficial changes. It will be suggested here that, on the contrary, the human condition and also the human understanding of its condition, do change much more fundamentally than theologians and men of religion commonly suppose; and that we shall not make much progress in religion and theology until the implications of this possibility are recognized.

(3) Once the fundamental inquiries so far suggested have been carried out, we should be in a position to examine more effectively any particular mode of piety presented to us as a valid means towards communion with God. Here too the mode and order of analysis is important so as to avoid confusion. In attempts at the renewal of piety there is a prevailing tendency to assume that at least the *object* of an act of worship or private discipline of piety is clear and agreed, and the discussion then centres on 'methods'. Yet this is often a mistaken procedure: the object is often *not* agreed or even examined, and hence arguments about methods often miss the point; and if the object *is* clear it may settle some of the methods or allow of a variety of

methods which in any case are of secondary importance in comparison with the object.

It may be suggested that what really need to be analysed with reference to any mode of spirituality are the following points:

(a) *The Aim:* that is, What model of Christianity is being assumed or chosen? Here fundamental theological differences are liable to emerge. Is the ultimate to be 'vision of God', 'communion with God', 'union with God'?[3] Is the process to whatever is aimed at to be conceived in terms of 'salvation' or 'discipleship'?[4] And if 'discipleship' (or for that matter the more traditional 'imitation') of Christ, what picture of Christ is in mind? – an ascetic world-denier or a 'man for others'? It will be suggested that much traditional piety has seen Christ's First Great Commandment as basic, 'love the Lord thy God', the implementation of the Second Commandment depending upon it; the models of 'vision of God' and 'communion with God' really both receive their content from this basic order of priorities. But much modern radical theology has inverted this order of priorities: the basic aim becomes the Second Commandment, while the great and First Commandment (if consciously considered at all) is seen as achieved by fulfilling the Second. But the content of the Second – and the view of Christianity and of Christ – turns out very often to be indistinguishable from an enlightened social benevolence without specifically Christian content. This will be discussed properly at a later stage; here the point is simply made that differences in 'aim' or 'model' do exist, ought to be recognized, and have far-reaching repercussions on spirituality. Certainly, this must be seen before any discussion on 'methods' can get anywhere.

(b) *The Types:* Under this head one thinks of such historic and contemporary contrasts in piety as those indicated by watchwords like 'Catholic or Protestant', 'Corporate or Individual', 'Sacramental or Non-Sacramental', 'Priestly or Prophetic' and a number of others. However tiresome and hackneyed they may seem, however much we may rightly refuse to regard them as mutually exclusive, they nevertheless reflect real contrasts and choices; and they may well turn out to be affected by the 'aim' or 'model' of Christian ideal which has already been chosen.

(c) *The Conditions:* By this is meant the conditions in which the appropriate spirituality for achieving the chosen 'aim' of Christianity may be or should be worked out. It is important to distinguish this category from that of 'means' (see below), if only because of the strong traditional contrast between the provision made in Catholic piety for the religious life lived in communities under rule and the absence of this ideal and of provision for it in Protestantism for most of its history. What is at stake here is not just means and techniques but the very nature and basis of the religious life. In the Catholic tradition there is implied the idea of what is sometimes critically referred to as a 'double standard': i.e. that the highest kind of spiritual life can best be worked out in a religious order, or at least in some adaptation of its rules for a life lived in the world. The traditional Protestant rejection of this has been explicitly on the grounds of a 'single standard' which is, moreover, to be that of a life lived in the world as the norm, one's 'worldly' vocation being in itself the condition of the highest Christianity if properly carried out. In saying this no attempt is made to judge one ideal or the other as preferable; but the contrast is real and important in that it helps to define the very different conditions under which different types of piety can hope to be observed.

(d) *The Means or Methods:* This category, though it could very well cover much that has been referred to under (b)

9

and (*c*), is here used mainly to refer to particular religious practices and techniques, e.g. of prayer and worship.

These distinctions have been made as aids to analysis and will be used particularly in the last chapter of this essay. The most fundamental distinction, it may be suggested, is that between the 'aim' or 'model' taken for the Christian life and the means adopted to achieve it. The category of 'conditions' under which the 'aim' is pursued may be seen as a kind of middle term linking the two because in some respects it is determined by the aim adopted, while it may also be an important part of the means by which the aim is pursued and within which particular 'types' and 'methods' of piety are practised.

The rest of this study will proceed on the following plan: In Chapter 2 some conditioning factors in religion will be discussed, particularly in the light of the question already raised about the possibility of religion being an activity which needs to be learnt. Chapter 3 describes the growth of the contrasting 'Catholic' and 'Protestant' traditions of piety and the problems faced by the latter in particular. It will be argued, however, that some of the main factors affecting contemporary spirituality are the result of developments since the late 18th century, and an attempt is made in Chapter 4 to explain how this has come about, with reference to external and internal pressures on Christianity and the spiritualities evolved in response to them. Chapter 5 is a systematic analysis of the problems and options for contemporary spirituality, considered in the light of the material described in the earlier chapters, and analysed according to the categories defined in the Introduction.

2. Conditioning Factors in Religion

1. Religion as 'Natural' or 'Acquired'

IN WHAT follows it should be understood that the question of a 'supernatural' agency in religion is not under discussion; it is assumed that it is possible to conceive of such an agency as operating by either of the means suggested by the title of this section.

(1) If religion is *natural* to man, this may mean one of two things:

(*a*) That man is by nature 'religious'. What does this mean? It might mean, as psychologists used to say, that man has a religious 'instinct' comparable to those of self-preservation, hunger and sex. Such language is less popular than it used to be, for the so-called 'religious' instinct seems in fact to be too complex and diverse to be attributed to a single motive.[1] Another possibility is to look at the matter institutionally: some sociologists (e.g. Arnold Gehlen) have suggested that human institutions (of which religious institutions are an example) may be regarded as regulatory agencies channelling human conduct, as the so-called instincts channel the behaviour of animals. The attempts made by theologians from Schleiermacher onwards to establish the existence of a specifically religious 'sense', so as to establish the universality and independence of religion have to meet psychological and sociological findings of the kind just mentioned. But there is a simpler test as well. If one points to the almost universal occurrence (in place and time) of religious activity, it must also be recognized that a single exception would invalidate the thesis. Then there is the apparent[2] decline of religion in the West in fairly recent times which might seem to cast doubt on religion as 'natural' to mankind. One answer to this might be that when men do not *appear* to be religious, they are nevertheless religious *in fact*; being (it is assumed) religious by nature, their religious 'instincts' are expressed either in religious forms of a new and unusual kind, or else in 'secular' substitutes (e.g. Nazism, Marxism, material aspirations, etc.). It would appear that modern attempts to renew religious practice really depend very often on assumptions of this kind. If religion seems to be declining, the argument seems to run, this may be expected to be a reversible process, religion being capable of revival on the basis of finding more acceptable 'religious' forms for instincts which have been temporarily diverted into other channels. A 'secular' variant of this view is that of Pareto and others[3] who have seen men as essentially irrational beings, whose emotions need and will find expression in all and any social circumstances. Worship is non-rational but has value as satisfying permanent emotional needs. If 'worship' in the normal sense declines, then the emotional needs will be fulfilled by some other means which may then be interpreted (if one so wishes) as 'religion'.

Whatever else may be said of the view of religion as natural, it may be pointed out that it raises an awkward problem from the psychological point of view. If religion is 'natural', then it is determined by compulsive instincts to serve unconscious needs other than the conscious meanings usually posited for religion. Hence religious behaviour is seen as 'a deceptive mask to mask a selfish gratification with respectability',[4] and the same might apply to religion seen as fulfilling purely sociological functions. Some further comments will be made on this problem at a later stage in this chapter.

(b) The other possible meaning of religion as 'natural' would be that though not every man has a religious instinct which is bound to be expressed either in religion or in some substitute for it, yet all men have a 'capacity' for religion which, under suitable conditions, may receive religion and make it a reality for the person concerned.[5] One still has to explain, however, why, even when all circumstances seem to be favourable, religion is nevertheless rejected.[6] On the other hand, unless some kind of 'capacity' for religion is posited, it is difficult to see how anyone ever becomes religious at all. The notion of capacity may then serve as a bridge from 'natural' to 'acquired' views of religion.

(2) If religion is '*acquired*' one must, presumably, have some such notion as that just mentioned – of men (at least some men) as possessing a capacity for religion even though this may not always be fulfilled by religion. In psychological terms[7] this may be taken to mean that religion is not reducible to a segmental drive like fear or to compulsive neurotic obsessions, but is a conscious intention arising out of a reasonable learning to respond to whatever is regarded as the divine or ultimate in life. (In fact this is to use the narrower

concept of 'learning' and in rather an intellectual sense: here the term 'acquired' has been preferred as more comprehensive. There are various ways and levels of 'acquiring'.) The criticism might be made of religion as 'acquired' that it is a superficial form of behaviour that imitates what others do, so as to conform, or have prestige, or win approval. Hence religion is optional and inessential to basic human needs. It may be pointed out, however, that even if this is true, the choice of religion may still be taken if a man so wishes, and there is nothing to prevent a man from orientating his life around this choice.

To sum up. By 'natural' is meant regarding religion as something in the permanent nature and need of mankind which nothing can fundamentally change; only the mode of expression can vary. This (it is admitted) may vary to the extent to which the channels of expression are of an apparently non-religious type.

By 'acquired', on the other hand, is meant that, at most, men have a 'capacity' for religion. Whether a man actually acquires religion depends on mental and emotional attitudes which are in their turn conditioned by society and by religious institutions which are themselves socially conditioned. Hence, if for any reason religious activities are frowned upon by society, if they become suspect intellectually and socially, if the 'need' for them is not promoted and evoked, then there nothing in the nature of man as such to make him 'religious'. This at least makes it possible to give a more plausible explanation of religious change, rise and decline; and of why men may in certain cases and at certain times not seem to 'need' religion in the sense which seems demanded by the idea of a permanent religious 'nature'. As Dr Bryan Wilson has pointed out, the latter view posits a universal and unchanging human psychology which takes little account of social change as changing men's emotional needs and responses.

Yet in fact modern Western men seem to act and think more rationally and over a wider area of experience than once they did. The nature of modern society, the effects of which have been progressively manifested at least since the Industrial Revolution, 'may alter man's emotional responses, and even his felt sense of emotional need: it may alter the age at which certain reassurances are sought, the circumstances in which they can be accepted and the degree to which they *must* be collective and institutionalized, or *may* be individual and (apparently rather than really) random. In particular, in a society where intellectual criteria dominate, it may well be that what cannot be intellectually accepted cannot be emotionally reassuring.' Wilson adds that modern men appear to suffer acutely from loss of emotional reassurance, but that religion appears no longer capable of providing this for the mass of men.[8]

The special application of this point of view to the contemporary situation will be discussed in more detail later, especially in connexion with the phenomenon of 'secularization'. For the moment it is sufficient to point out the implications of a 'learnt' view of religion for the whole of the present study. One major effect is that the history of religion and indeed the general development of mankind, and the effects of both kinds of development on the meaning and practice of religion, are taken seriously: that is, development and change and the possibility of really new situations and therefore really radical reform are taken seriously. It has already been suggested that much 'reform' on the basis of religion being 'natural' to man does not really do this. Consequently one finds that, for example, projects for the renewal of worship and spirituality tend to assume that corporate worship, and particular forms of corporate worship, can be recalled from the past with a minimum of 'translation'. It is assumed, moreover, that once

15

the translation is done, man's worshipping instinct will inevitably recall him to the reformed pattern. If, however, human nature is more changeable than this, more responsive to permanent social and psychological change, and if worship and much else in religion have to be learnt and acquired, then the processes of historical change are of great importance; and so are the circumstances in which learning and acquiring religion may be able to take place.

It is in the light of these considerations that considerable attention is paid in this essay to the way in which historical, psychological and sociological factors deeply affect the options for spirituality open to us today.

2. Some Conditioning Factors in 'Acquired' Religion

From one point of view it might be argued that a major conditioning factor (particularly for modern religion) is *intellectual*. This is easily misunderstood and even dismissed if it is taken to mean what affects only an intellectual minority and may only be a small part even of their religious motivation. What is meant here, however, is the 'mental' element in religion: never absent even in the least 'intellectual' of men; an increasing factor for an increasing number of people at the present time even as a purely 'intellectual' affair. Moreover, it cannot be too strongly emphasized that as a consciously intellectual factor, and as a more diffused attitude of mind, deriving from the dissemination of intellectual attitudes and theories (as with 'evolution' and psychology) into the common unconscious bias of the modern outlook, this factor in religion is of great importance. What these intellectual attitudes are and how they affect spirituality will be considered later. The point to make at once – and it may be applied particularly to what will be said in a moment about psychology and sociology –

is that there are at least three ways in which intellectual changes affect religious attitudes.

In the first place, the actual forces described as operating by such studies as psychology and sociology must be recognized as existing and effective, whatever particular theories about them are put forward and believed in; and whether or not (as applied to religion) they are regarded as 'complete' explanations of religious phenomena. Secondly, the very fact that such studies and theories are current means that people are more or less conscious of such factors being invoked in connexion with religion, and this insensibly affects religious attitudes. For example, whatever the truth of evolution and Freud's theories, once they are known they make it impossible to make a simple appeal to the story of the Fall or to religious experience in the same way as before; and this is by no means true for 'intellectuals' only. Finally, if psychological and sociological and other factors in religion are recognized, this has one particularly important implication for spirituality: it points very forcibly to a conscious spirituality involving a high degree of self-understanding, while at the same time it provides some of the tools to make this possible; this is particularly true of *psychology*. The wider importance of this subject has already been indicated in the discussion of religion as natural or acquired. Here it may be added (and this applies to all the 'conditioning factors') that in contemporary religion it is more than ever necessary that religious observance should conform as far as possible to actual religious understanding and experience: the gap between the two is one underlying reason for the contemporary crisis of spirituality.

A final note may be added on the *sociological* approach, though what is said of this would apply equally well, so far as status and limits in relation to religion are concerned, to other 'secular' assessments of religious phenomena. Such an approach passes no judgement on the question of the theological aspects of religion: 'That theological meanings are also socially evolved and perhaps socially determined is probably as near as the sociologist might wish to come to the discussion of theological issues. Churches are social institutions; men's conceptions of God are socially prescribed (and even protestations against those conceptions bear no less the mark of the social situation in which they arise). But the measure of the truth of these conceptions, or the legitimacy of these institutions in relation to some posited supermundane order, pass beyond . . . sociological concern.'[9] Sociology, therefore, regards religion as primarily an institutional phenomenon, and this of course may leave it possible to consider other dimensions of religion from other points of view; or even to make distinctions between institutional religion and 'real' religion, of which institutional religion might be regarded as at best only a partial embodiment. On the other hand, it seems clear that the general institutional situation, and the factors which affect institutions, must affect religion itself even if the distinction just mentioned is made. In practice it is difficult for the sociologist and the theologian to avoid overlapping, as Wilson's book shows. We shall see this later in the discussion of 'secularization'; for here, as in other sociological discussions of religion, it becomes apparent that once the sociology of religion gets beyond mere sociography (the collection of church attendance statistics and the like) and proceeds to the discussion of the Church in the light of institutional theory – still more when the inquiry concerns the nature of subjective religiosity as shaped by social factors – the nature of religion (and of spirituality not least) is involved. The present writer can only repeat his conviction that no adequate discussion of modern spirituality can or ought to attempt to evade these issues.

3. Catholic and Protestant Traditions in Spirituality

IN THIS chapter I shall be referring in the main to the development of these two main traditions in Western Christendom up to and including the 18th century. As I shall attempt to show in the next chapter, the decisive changes which began to be evident from about that time make it reasonable to divide the material in this way.

1. The Catholic Tradition

There is a sense in which the Catholic tradition, particularly before the Reformation, has included within itself most conceivable varieties of aim and method in Christian spirituality. It is possible, nevertheless, to make significant contrasts between the dominant traditions within Catholicism and those within Protestantism during the period we are now considering.

The ultimate aim might be defined as that of achieving

such a measure of actual holiness as to fit one for communion with God: perhaps, in the case of the exceptional personality, to the point of an actual momentary vision of him in this life; or perhaps a total and almost unmediated union with him. How far, and in what sense, these highest flights of piety are possible has always been a matter of controversy, and obviously something much lower in degree was to be expected of the generality of people. Still, it would appear that the ideal for all would be the achievement of a greater or lesser degree of actual holiness in conformity to the life of Christ, and seen in terms of the stripping off of vices, the putting on of virtues. Ideally, again, this involves the notion of an absolute concentration upon God and a turning away from the world and men and the self at least for the higher levels of spirituality: a concentration upon the First rather than the Second Great Commandment in the last resort. The ideal is essentially a world-denying one. Theologically, the process may be seen as one in which the will of man co-operates with the will of God, grace progressively perfecting nature.

The conditions under which this aim may be achieved are affected by the aim itself and by the degree to which particular types of men may be expected to achieve it. Total concentration upon God and a world-denying holiness would seem in practice to involve the kind of detachment from worldly connexions which can only be achieved in an individual or communal life physically separated from ordinary life. Those still involved in ordinary life can only hope for a lower approximation to the ideal. It is for this reason that the notion of 'two standards' for the spiritual life develops. The two ways are described at an early stage by the 4th-century historian Eusebius, as follows[1]:

Therefore there hath been instituted in the Church of Christ, two ways, or manners, of living. The one, raised above the ordinary state of nature, and common ways of living, rejects wedlock, possessions, and worldly goods, and, being wholly separate and removed from the ordinary conversation of common life, is appreciated and devoted solely to the worship and service of God, through an exceeding degree of heavenly love.

They who are of this order of people seem dead to the life of this world, and, having their bodies only upon earth, are in their minds, and contemplations, dwelling in heaven. From whence, like so many heavenly inhabitants, they look down upon human life, making intercessions and oblations to Almighty God for the whole race of mankind . . . with the highest exercises of true piety, with cleansed and purified hearts, and with a whole form of life strictly devoted to virtue. These are their sacrifices, which they continually offer unto God, imploring His mercy and favour for themselves and their fellow-creatures.

Christianity receives this as the perfect manner of life.

The other is of a lower form, and, suiting itself more to the condition of human nature, admits of chaste wedlock, the care of children and family, of trade and business, and goes through all the employments of life under a sense of piety, and fear of God.

Now they who have chosen this manner of life, have their set times for retirement and spiritual exercises, and particular days are set apart for their hearing and learning the word of God. And this order of people is considered as in the second state of piety.

The matter can, however, be looked at in a rather different way. Spiritual writers have often talked about a distinction between the 'contemplative' and the 'active' life. The 'active' life is not so much a matter of merely living in the world of work as of doing necessary business together with positive good works and moral conduct. The 'contemplative' life is 'to retain indeed with all one's mind the love of God and neighbour, but to rest from exterior action, and cleave only to the desire of the Maker, that the mind . . . may be aglow to see the face of its Creator'.[2] Gregory the Great, from whom this quotation is taken, saw contemplation as open to all in all stations in life, not merely to a few specialists or gifted souls. He was, indeed, prepared to see a

'mixed' life of contemplation *and* active good works and
virtue as the best of all, but he seems to see this as most
likely to be practised by preachers rather than by ordinary
Christians:

> The excellence of preachers is far above that of the continent and
> silent, and the eminence of the continent outdistances greatly that
> of married people. The married, though they do well and desire to
> see God, yet are occupied by domestic cares and are divided in mind.
> . . . But preachers not only withhold themselves from vices, but . . .
> instruct [others] in the pursuit of holy living. Yet there is for all
> three the same faith, the same reward of everlasting life, the same
> joy in the vision of God.[3]

At the risk of over-simplifying one may therefore say
that the conditions of the spiritual life vary as follows.
There is life in a religious order: an enclosed order of
greater or lesser strictness, more or less cut off from the
world; or an order living under rule but committed to
a variety of activities in the world and therefore less able to
concentrate on pure contemplation. There is life as a priest:
in this case performing functions in the world, not subject
to rule in the same sense as the first but nevertheless separated from the laity by orders, celibacy and work, and following some modification of monastic spiritual discipline.
Finally, there are the laity: here too there is more than one
possibility – from the acceptance of such a modification of
monastic rule as is possible to a layman in the world (including voluntary celibacy) down to the minimum observance of the Church's public worship and of the discipline
of confession and Holy Communion. (It may be observed
that Eusebius saw the 'second' and 'lower' way of spiritual
life as at its best including periods of 'retreat', during which,
in effect, one temporarily observed monastic piety in the
world; and this seems essential if any approximation to the

ideal of a life directed to concentration on God and a denial of the world is to be upheld.)

The means used to achieve the stated ends vary in certain respects according to the level of piety aimed at. In general, methods depend on the view of grace and salvation already described, and in large measure, especially at the level of ordinary and popular piety, it may be said without prejudice that 'spiritual' ends are seen as strongly aided by 'physical' sacramental means. In what follows it should be stressed that I have in mind more particularly the system as it operated at the time of the Reformation, but the principles involved – I am less concerned with abuses – continued to operate afterwards. Through baptism one was seen as cleansed from original sin and given an infusion of grace; the subsequent perpetual relapse into actual sins could be and should be dealt with by various sacramental means, notably by sacramental confession and the Eucharist, which purge sin and provide grace from God through the ministry of the priest and with the co-operation of the believer. The same principle lay behind the other sacraments and also the other means of grace such as pilgrimages, penances, relics, indulgences and the work of chantries: they supplemented and at times perhaps almost supplanted the more central means of grace – the Mass itself before the Reformation more often conveying grace by adoration than by communion. In general (and allowing for corruptions) the system conformed theologically to the more precisely defined theology enunciated at the Council of Trent, after the Reformation had begun. That is to say, a man was seen as progressively 'justified' in the sense of being made actually holy, by working off sin and working on righteousness; this not by his own sole efforts, but rather by the co-operation of his will and efforts with the initiating and sustaining grace of God. Thus grace was infused in him

23

to make him righteous. Moreover, the work of Christ and of the saints was seen, at least in the simplified popular theology of the early 16th century, as making available a 'treasury' of their surplus merits for the benefit of sinners. This could be tapped by means of indulgences granted (by this time) in return for minimal acts of penance – and even by proxy for the dead to save them like oneself from some of the pains of purgatory.[4] The indulgence system, however distasteful it may now seem to be, was both logical and necessary, given the existing theory of salvation; for, if salvation is essentially a continual process of 'justification' in the sense given above (i.e. the making of men actually holy by grace in co-operation with our will), and if, by definition, no one is perfectly holy and capable of the complete vision of God in this life, then it follows that the process must continue for a greater or lesser period after death, in purgatory, before heaven is attained.

It would be hard to find any serious Protestant historian who would now wish to deny that positive Catholic reform in doctrine and life took place in the 16th century, and that this so-called 'Counter-Reformation' was not merely a negative response to the Protestant Reformation (however much the doctrinal definitions of Trent were conditioned by the questions raised by Protestants) but had also independent Catholic origins. None the less, it needs to be stressed that, so far as doctrine and the spirituality based on it are concerned, Catholic reform in this period was substantially an attempt (largely successful) to purify and revivify traditional patterns and assumptions; and this in spite of signs of some Catholic reformers wanting more. The theology of Trent has already been referred to. In worship the Mass remained in Latin, communion remained in one kind and infrequent, the reform of the Missal and Breviary was conservative. The remarkable advent of new religious orders (notably the Jesuits) and of mysticism (notably in Spain with St Teresa and St John of the Cross) and the appearance of St Ignatius Loyola's *Spiritual Exercises* are without question major events in the history of spirituality, not to say in secular history. But it must still be insisted that they are further developments in an existing Catholic tradition of piety: the Jesuit ideal, for example, is still that of the religious order under rule while active in the world.

In the 17th century some strains and problems in Catholic piety become more evident. Following on some of the questions debated at Trent, the Jansenist controversy in France showed that the legacy of St Augustine and the problem of grace and freewill affected Catholics as well as Protestants, though it was the Tridentine form of compromise that prevailed in the end. The effects of this type of controversy could be seen in the quarrels of the Jansenists and others over questions of casuistry in dealing with penitents (a problem which also troubled contemporary Protestant ministers, as we shall see). The problem of absolute perfection and 'pure love' was debated in the case of Fénelon and others; and this, again, had a Protestant parallel in Wesley in the 18th century, and involves the question of the very aim of spirituality as such. As to the conditions under which, and the means by which, it is to be pursued, one may simply mention the cases of St François de Sales and St Vincent de Paul. Both illustrate the continuing problems of what kind of spirituality can and should be pursued by laymen in the world: in these men one sees further attempts at the cultivation of the inner individual life in 'worldly' conditions and side by side with the development of the more 'active' life of charitable and social service. But of all this it may still be said that what one sees is a further exploration and adaptation of the traditional aims, conditions and methods of Catholic spirituality. The same may be said of 'new' devotions like that to the Sacred Heart and of the 'theatrical' approach to the Liturgy which modern Catholics have criticized.[5]

This last example might be taken as a sign of the coming secularization of religious life. In the period of the 18th-century Enlightenment one is certainly impressed by the extent to which traditional assumptions and patterns of piety, both corporate and individual, continued as they had during the Middle Ages. In some respects they developed further – one may cite the example of St Alfonso Liguori's devotion to the Immaculate Conception. The hold of religious observance, if only as a customary ritual pattern, continued at any rate until the French Revolution: a vivid picture of this kind of Catholic society may be seen in the study of Angers ecclesiastical society by Professor McManners.[6] But of this society it has been said that it was 'a religious society just secular enough to give hearing to Enlightenment ideas, just pious enough to cause friction'.[7] In fact the content of religion and the relation of religion to thought and society in the 18th century was beginning in some quarters to show signs of change, if not as decisively and extensively in Catholicism as in Protestantism. Catholics, like Protestants, answered sceptical attacks on Christianity by innocently adopting some of the rationalistic assumptions of the sceptics;[8] at the level of preaching there is a shift in religious rhetoric 'from a rather grim Augustinian emphasis on hell and damnation in 17th-century sermons to the bland modern emphasis on good Christian living in 18th-century sermons'.[9]

This was accompanied by other signs of secularization in the sense of the decline of strictly ecclesiastical power and the growth in the power and claims over religion of the secular authorities in Catholic as in Protestant countries. A new and, from the Church's point of view, sinister phase in this process appeared in the phenomenon of 'Josephinism' in Austria and similar activities in Tuscany. This was, from one point of view, the attempt of 'enlightened' monarchs to extend rational (and royal) control over human affairs in the true 18th-century manner. Behind the specific reforms one can discern an attempt to remodel the Church and its piety on political and moral principles conforming to contemporary ideas of rational religion: superstition and indeed the supernatural are to be ruled out. Hence religious toleration, the closing of religious houses unless they were 'useful' for medical or educational purposes (those for contemplation were useless and superstitious from this point of view). Seminaries were to train priests in modern thinking instead of scholastic theology; saints' days and pilgrimages were reduced. In Tuscany the process was extended to worship and included attacks on the popular cult of the Sacred Heart, on indulgences, on the more archaic features of the Breviary, and on the idea of Transubstantiation. This was not a belated manifestation of Reformation Protestantism, but the 18th-century attack on supernatural, irrational religion: the significance of this for traditional Catholic spirituality is obvious, for it attacks its aims, institutions and methods together. To complete the picture, one may add that the French Revolution quickly developed an even more fundamental attack – on Christianity as such, with some attempts to replace it with other cults.

The results and significance of all this will appear later. One may anticipate by saying that the upshot, in the 19th century, was neither the demise nor even the drastic revision of Catholicism in the manner that might have been expected. The Revolution provoked conservative reactions politically and religiously; and traditional religious ideals actually revived and strengthened in important respects. All the same, a warning of what must eventually come had

27

been issued; the divorce between Catholicism and the modern world began; the Church's hold on society was weakened, particularly in the aspect of religion as a universal social ritual.

2. The Protestant Tradition

It is certainly no less difficult to sum up Protestantism in all its variety in a page or two than to characterize Roman Catholicism in brief without distortion.

While the religious aim of Protestantism might in one sense be said to resemble that of Catholicism and all Christianity, namely, to attain communion with God, the conception of this was different. The basic theological difference centred upon the doctrine of justification in the Reformation period, and for Protestants this was clearly something more than a protest against incidental weaknesses in medieval piety which later Catholicism cleared up. The Council of Trent endeavoured to avoid too great a stress on men's own efforts to righteousness while avoiding also the annihilation of all human effort and co-operation with God. For Trent 'justification' was a process of growth in *actual* holiness and not a once-for-all act or status. For Protestants, it was more of a God-given status of forgiveness and acceptance conferred by the immediate gracious act of God in consideration of the work of Christ, the only truly holy man. To say that a man was 'justified' said nothing about his actual holiness; to assert too much about this was to open oneself to the risk of believing that one's own efforts (even 'assisted' by or 'co-operating' with God) had somehow earned God's favour. The strength of this position was that it conferred immediate communion with God rather than postponing this to the end of a lifelong and imperfect process of growth, and at the same time did away with anxieties about the inadequacies of repentance barring one from God's presence; for it was not our own achievement but the immediate grace of God on which acceptance and communion for ever depended. Hence, as will be seen in a moment, the whole Catholic apparatus of a mediating priesthood, of a sacramental system, of merits and purgatory was essentially unnecessary. On the basis of a Scriptural criterion over against what were felt to be the false accretions of tradition, much of that old system was dismissed as not only worthless but dangerous, and simplified means of grace were substituted for it. The weakness of the Protestant position (from which many consequences followed) was that it lay open to the charge of a legal fiction: the 'imputed righteousness' of Christ covered a man actually still unholy – a man, moreover, lacking any real incentive to become holy, perhaps positively discouraged from thinking he *could* become holy in any real sense. Lutherans, in particular, distrusted any theology which might seem to impugn the sovereign rights of justification by faith alone, fearing to return to the trust in human works of a 'corrupt' Catholicism. Calvinists, more obviously concerned in theology and practice to develop a holy Christian community, nevertheless suffered from their more precise commitment to predestination – another safeguard for reliance solely on the grace of God for salvation against all saving works by men. This seemed to cut the nerve of moral endeavour. It is a matter of historical fact that although such embarrassments as 'sinning that grace may abound' did occur, the Protestants were on the whole successful in establishing churches in which a positive and disciplined Christian life was possible. Nevertheless, the theological bases of a life progressing in holiness were not easy to establish, and we shall see that this accounts for a number of Protestant problems in spirituality. Other difficulties followed from the next subject to be considered – the conditions under which any holy life is to be pursued.

For Protestantism there was to be only one setting and only one standard of Christian life; the old distinctions between active and contemplative life, between a piety pursued in or out of the world, were abandoned and indeed attacked as improper and illusory. Monasticism and the 'religious' life in the technical Catholic sense were done away with, so were all the lay approximations to this, involving rules, vows and celibacy. So, for the ordinary laity, was the full scope of the priestly, sacramental and penitential system. Instead, there was one standard for all – that of Christian vocation pursued in one's 'worldly' calling and in marriage and the home. This exalted secular and, above all, family life as the highest kind of spiritual status. The family becomes a kind of microcosm of the Church; the priesthood of all believers, properly understood, is not merely a depreciation of separate priestly status but a positive obligation laid on every man to act as a priest for other men. But the question might be asked, as Kierkegaard asked it after seeing what Protestantism had become by the 19th century, whether this raised or lowered the standard of spirituality for all.[10] For the high Protestant aim of exalting the righteousness of God and making it available freely to all in the world was certainly not meant to relax the demands of God on men to concentrate on his will; nor was it meant to replace this with an active, secular concentration on the fulfilment of the Second Great Commandment; nor did it for a long time. But in the very long run (not simply, it is true, as a result of weaknesses inherent in the original Protestant position but certainly helped by them) this was one result.

The points made so far may be further illustrated from

the means which Protestants established for cultivating their 'Christianity in the world'. In some respects the results of Reformation principles were rather less drastic here than might have been expected, though they varied considerably through the new ecclesiastical spectrum: from Anglicans and Lutherans to the more drastic efforts of Calvinists, and on to the radical Anabaptists and the English Dissenters of the 17th century. All maintained a visible Church (though differing on how far and in what sense this was to be identified with the body of justified believers). All maintained a ministry (though no longer the essential mediating priesthood of Catholicism). All maintained some of the traditional means of grace (though many were cut out and all fell short of the sacramental status understood by Catholicism). But what, more positively, should be the ideal of spirituality, above all of the greatly enhanced status of lay spirituality? That was far more uncertain, and remained (as we shall see) a fundamental Protestant problem.

Much depended on public worship, which varied considerably in detail but shared certain common features. Above all, the Reformers started from a horror of the Mass and its accompanying doctrines of sacrifice and transubstantiation: one feels that the Reformers were far more successful in filling their followers with a horror of the Mass than in inculcating a positive valuation of the Protestant Communion which replaced it. There were certainly at work here other factors not specifically associated with the Protestant Reformation. But the fact remains that men like Luther and Calvin and Cranmer were disappointed of their ideal of a weekly celebration of the Lord's Supper as a Scriptural sacrament involving the communion of the people, in place of the quasi-magical spectacle of the medieval Mass. Protestants before long reduced it to a more occasional and less central act than this. Instead, they carried

31

on and even heightened the importance of one element in the medieval tradition, preaching, which became a major feature of much Protestant worship. Along with this, as a further infusion of Scriptural knowledge and practice, were public prayers, which varied from the relatively conservative Anglican Prayer Books to the barer forms of Calvinists and the English Puritans of the more extreme type.

All of this points to a more or less drastic purging of the more tangible, sacramental, physical symbols and means of grace seen as conveying the supernatural and realizing communion with God. This is, again, most obvious in the treatment of the Mass; though the purging in theory and practice varied from the high views of Luther through Anglicanism to the virtually memorialist view of Zwingli. The prevailing infrequency of communion in Protestantism shows the change from Catholicism, particularly when it is recalled that no Eucharist at all was held unless there were communicants. Public worship, then, centred on the Word, read, prayed and preached; and through the Word was to be mediated the main impact of God's work on the worshipper.

Then again, the Catholic discipline of the religious order had been abolished, and the discipline of the laity by church courts and more intimately through the confessional had been much altered. Calvin's and Beza's Geneva was probably the most effective of the Protestant attempts at a discipline for the whole church – more effective than Catholic canon law in producing the face of a Christian commonwealth. Anglicans did less well, and one element in the Puritan attempts to reform the Establishment was to improve it as the agency for a kingdom of God on earth, in this direction. The failure of all the Protestant states to keep up (or in some cases, as in England, ever to attain) that height of discipline led to other expedients, as we shall see. The point is not that they did worse than Catholics but rather that they failed to achieve the kind of universal lay piety which was the ideal, to replace the double standard of piety implied in the Catholic system.

The same may be said of more personal and private spirituality. The Catholic system has already been described: it depended on the basic Catholic theology of grace, and was worked out with the help of the priesthood, sacraments, confessional and the devotions associated with the Mass. The Protestants had really destroyed all these. The centre of Protestant devotion was really, once again, the Word: the Word driven home beyond public worship by catechizing and other instruction; private Bible study; private prayer – ideally, the cultivation of an intense and continuing personal awareness of God's demands, mercy and forgiveness; the working out of obedience in one's worldly calling. The Protestant Churches all made attempts in this direction with varying success.[11] But the strain of a religion which by its nature seems to be that of the intense minority, yet was attempted for the conforming majority often in a State Church in Protestant countries, appears to have been too great in the long run. As the social ritual of the majority in an established religious social order, it lacked much of the immemorial physical symbolism of Catholicism, as we have seen, and lacked too that Church's popular devotional resources.

In sum, the Protestant abolition of the two standards with the possibility of a very explicit renunciation of the world in the monastic sense, together with the exaltation of the layman's calling in the world as the standard of all, meant that the minimum standard of expectation for a lay spirituality had been raised. At the same time, the heights of Catholic sanctity of a world-denying kind, involving an absolute concentration on God for himself alone, had been abandoned in theory and practice. The actual content of a Protestant piety practised in the world was not sufficiently precise, nor were the means to achieve it. Failure here was liable to lead to an acceptance in the end of the prevailing standards of secular society and to an eventual relaxing of the ideal of concentration on God to a concentration on men. It is not suggested that this happened all at once or that when it did happen it was solely due to inherent weaknesses in Protestant principle. But one theological point may be made in this connexion. The tremendous emphasis on justification by grace through faith and the horror of salvation by 'works' did hinder an adequate development of positive teaching on sanctification, its content and methods.

It is therefore not surprising that, as Gordon Rupp put it,[12] the men of the century from, say, 1560 to 1660 added to the original Protestant emphasis on the two dimensions of the Church (Word and Sacrament) a concern for a 'third dimension', that of discipline. This is true of much in Catholicism as well; but the Protestant necessity was even more pressing. It was expressed at one level in the necessary development of State churches and of church organization generally; but also in attempts by these or other means to inculcate a 'Scriptural' discipline for the ends of piety. One version of this was (as has already been said) the attempt of the Puritans.[13] Another was the Laudian school of churchmen in 17th-century England who in their theology and piety often appear as a kind of mild approximation to reformed Catholicism.[14] They fell short in this period, however, of a restoration of religious orders, but, undoubtedly in such divines as Lancelot Andrewes or Jeremy Taylor, they recovered much private spiritual discipline of a Catholic type, together with the sanctification theology which underlies it.

The Puritans are more interesting. Although Calvinistic

Puritans (like other Calvinists on the Continent) show disquiet and therefore subtle modifications in their teaching of predestination, a doctrine which might seem not only morally intolerable but also morally paralysing, they tried to build their discipline of piety firmly on the foundation of justification by faith, the Protestant palladium. This, as Gordon Wakefield has pointed out,[15] is one way of distinguishing between the Protestant teachers of casuistry and spirituality in this period, and superficially similar Catholic teachings. Puritan spirituality is one which starts with men *already* justified, fully in a 'state of grace'. There are other distinctive features too: for example, Perkins's 'greatest case of conscience that ever was', whether a man is one of the elect or not (the great Calvinist problem). Or there is the theme of the spiritual pilgrimage (immortalized in the *Pilgrim's Progress*) which is a kind of Protestant counterpart to the Catholic 'ladder of perfection'.[16] Above all there is the continuing search for a non-monastic piety: in the world, lay, familial, tending to be activist.[17]

This last theme, which has implications both for theology and for spirituality, continues in various forms in the history of both English and Continental Protestantism in the period from the middle of the 17th century and well into the 18th century. The 'Catholic' element in Anglican piety already referred to dwindled rather rapidly (partly for political reasons) at the turn of the century – the celebrated William Law is a late survival. Here was the theme of a holiness wrought through the sacraments with the co-operation of the mortified will, expressed partly in good works. This last point is an element in the book whose title has been taken to epitomize English rational piety of the 18th century: *The Whole Duty of Man*. Yet this in fact emanated from High Church circles before 1660 and illustrates the complicated way in which a piety of duty done in this world could develop. The main stream of Anglican piety in that period inherited the Prayer Book and rather occasional Eucharists as the relic of the Catholic past and a certain barrier against a religion totally devoid of ritual and symbolism, though preaching became increasingly prominent.

Anglicanism in this period did attempt a practical and social holiness of an 'in-worldly' kind: it was not really an inner holiness of the Catholic type which, as has been said, was now evaporating. We may cite Robert Boyle, scientist and Anglican layman, as an example of a trend.[18] He saw piety as a constant attempt 'to make the world both a library and an oratory', 'moralising common incidents and common things' to encourage recollection and awareness of the further implications of day-to-day events and situations. Hence one made the world 'a school for rational souls to learn the knowledge of God' and 'every creature turn a preacher'. The Religious Societies from the 1670s and other moral and charitable organizations of the period testify to the desire for an organized and more intense lay piety, while they also indicate the increasing understanding of this in terms of good works – and the more dubious social end, in some instances, of the moral and religious discipline of the lower classes. Many roads in fact pointed to the development of what is often taken to be the characteristic religious line of the 18th century – a religion of prudential morality and duty: according to Evangelicals like Whitefield (who attacked Archbishop Tillotson's influential published sermons which were of this type), a total reversal of the fundamental truth of justification by faith.

Mention of Whitefield brings us to the verge of the Evangelical Revival; but to complete the picture of Protestant development up to that point it is as well to glance at one development on the Continent: Pietism and then its special offshoot of Moravianism. The point of these movements is that they represent within the Lutheran tradition yet another example of the consciousness of the theological incompleteness of the excessive preaching of justification by faith, and the practical defects of Protestant piety. The founder of Pietism, P. J. Spener, had predecessors in his approaches to a renewal of piety[19] but his *Pia Desideria* was a clear statement of the lines on which such a renewal should proceed. Viewed theologically, Spener shows the shift in Protestantism from a preoccupation with justification[20] to a concern for sanctification; from what Christ has done 'for' us, too easily seen in juridical and external terms, to what Christ must do 'in' us, in personal and moral terms. Spener saw himself as working out the practical implications of the Lutheran justification by faith as a 'new birth' with works expressive of it; and as encouraging the institutional expression of this in a more active lay piety. His 'collegia pietatis', Bible study and devotional groups, were part of a really determined attempt to develop a Protestant holiness in the world, of the ordinary laity in ordinary secular life, not subject to the notion of 'two standards'. From another point of view they have been accused of doing just this – creating a double standard and dividing the Church by an *ecclesiola in ecclesia*.[21]

There are other examples of such attempts: Labadie, the Calvinist, in Holland is one. The mixture of mysticism and personal religion, the cultivation of sanctification, the use of groups which characterizes these movements, may best be interpreted as signs of a continuing search for a real Protestant piety of holiness and the means to achieve it. A remarkable example of this is the case of Zinzendorf and the Moravians. Here there are the special features of a shift to a specifically (at times sentimentally) Christocentric religion; a concern for personal conversion; and a set of institutions amounting to a quasi-monastic community under an autocratic head. It is, however, a Protestant 'monastery', i.e. of married as well as single people, living in the domestic setting of (in some cases) a self-contained community for all secular as well as sacred purposes. But it was also an evangelistic and missionary agency; thus, the holiness is really of a Protestant rather than a Catholic type in practice as well as theology.

From one point of view Moravianism may be seen as part of the movement of 'Evangelical Revival' which stretched from New England to Germany and included a variety of groups in Britain.[22] From the point of view of spirituality all were advocates of 'real' and 'heart' religion as against merely 'formal' religion; most of them were concerned in one way or another with salvation by faith as against salvation by works; most of them had also some concern with the problem of holiness; and most of them showed a concern with what has been called[23] the 'fourth dimension' of 'Christian fellowship' added to the three aspects of Word, sacrament and discipline already mentioned in connexion with the piety derived from the Reformation. Nevertheless, within this common set of concerns there are important differences; and the significance of the movement may be seen by examining it briefly on the side of theology and ideals, then on the side of the institutions embodying these ideals.[24]

Theology and ideals. On the face of it this was a reaction from what was felt to be an over-rationalized and over-moralized religious system back to the Reformation emphasis on revelation in Scripture and the doctrine of justification by faith. At the same time it was an upholding of the religion of the heart, of experience, of conversion: 'real' against 'formal' religion. But beyond this point the Revival split. Anglican Calvinist Evangelicals held to predestination and suspected any claim to real and progressive inherent holiness achieved in this life. Wesley and his followers preached a universal possibility of salvation conditional on men's response, and held out the ideal of a progressive and real growth in holiness to the point even of a so-called 'perfection' in this life. This for Wesley was the true end of religion to which justification was only in the last resort a means; it was, as he expounded it, a fresh and surprising mutation in Protestantism which probably owes a debt not only to the Anglican but also to the Roman tradition. (One may possibly compare Wesley's controversial view of a perfection which may be caught in a moment with Fénelon's 'amour pur'.[25]) Thus Wesley in the limited circles in which he was operating took up a number of contemporary possibilities in religion – reason and moral endeavour; grace and faith; justification and sanctification. Particularly significant is the post-Reformation concern for an actual holiness which should not be mere morality, merely human and limited; a holiness of the laity in common life yet also under discipline; and a holiness of 'inward tempers' and concentration on God as well as man. The weakness of all this lay in the vagueness with which the holiness was conceived; the failure to convince even his followers of the possibility of perfection in a moment; and the failure to capture more than a small section of English religious life.

Institutions. Anglican Evangelicalism[26] limited its own scope in the long run by its refusal to abandon or modify the parish system and ordinary means of grace provided within it; it depended, moreover, on clerical efforts *for* the laity rather than co-operative efforts *by* the laity for themselves. Wesley too wished to work within the system, but circumstances conspired with his fundamental conviction that his task was to spread 'Scriptural holiness' and that all else, including church order, unusual means of grace and lay helpers, were means to this end. He therefore broke Anglican 'order', though without accepting the fact that he had broken with the Anglican Church. While insisting that his organization and expedients were to supplement and not supplant Anglican provisions, Wesley had in fact created a coherent and self-perpetuating movement with its own sources of religious satisfaction and what soon became a new self-contained Church.

The difficulties that have always been found in classifying and interpreting Methodism in the history of Protestantism derive from the special nature of Wesley's original ideal which does not conform easily to Protestant categories up to that time: the well-known aphorism about a 'necessary synthesis of the Protestant ethic of grace and the Catholic ethic of holiness' at least points to the nature of the problem and (less certainly) to the nature of Wesley's solution. What we have here is perhaps the last major attempt for a fairly substantial section of people within the fully Protestant world and largely within a Protestant type of theology, to create a Protestant spirituality which takes Scripture alone and justification by faith alone seriously; but at the same time an attempt to develop a doctrine of real and progressive and inward holiness, concentrating on God as its object, and to be worked out in the world even if with its mind on things above. In terms of spirituality the question for Protestantism had always been whether Protestantism could develop a spirituality to replace that of Catholicism, the rejection of which at the Reformation had been one of the original Protestant movement's most decisive breaks with the past. Even the High Churchmen of the 17th century failed to recapture the full Catholic pattern to which they in some sense aspired, and they failed in any case to capture their Church (a failure repeated in the 19th century). The exclusion of the Mass affected both public and private piety, and the liturgy and sermon had to suffice as norm: the former preserved a public Protestant penitential for the average man, and the latter was an instrument for the cultivation of a relatively relaxed religious morality in the world. The results by the 18th century worked against the kind of progress in holiness pursued by some measure of renunciation of the world, implicit in Catholic piety and institutionalized in monasticism.

Wesley and Methodism fit into this Protestant framework and Protestant problem, both in what they attempted and in what they did not attempt to do. The religion Wesley developed was not essentially 'sacramental', despite much that has been said on this matter.[27] The place taken by the Mass and its accompaniments in the total pattern of Catholic piety was, and had to be, filled for Methodists with a variety of means of grace. And the supervision of these was entrusted to laymen. But Wesley, while rejecting the monastic inculcation of piety, tried to make a Protestant substitute (as the Moravians had in a different way). He set up the ideal of holiness moving to perfection; he saw the setting for this as provided in his Bands and Societies which were graded originally in accordance with the degree of religious achievement, but without complete social withdrawal, for the members were fully in the world. The system of examination in these groups provided a mutual Protestant confessional. The more ascetic elements in Wesley (including criticism of female finery and male prosperity) provided even an element of 'renunciation', which, indeed, the whole system tended to foster.

But Wesley really failed. The Methodists, including the preachers, rejected Wesley's doctrine of instantaneous perfection and failed to develop the rest of his perfection doctrine. They failed to maintain the more intense inner groups of those pursuing perfection most explicitly. The movement as a whole failed to maintain the societary pursuit of a Protestant holiness in the circumstances of a developing Church.[28] This particular movement has been cited rather fully simply because it demonstrates in a dramatic way some of the underlying problems of a Protestant spirituality. Could a holiness as intense as that of Wesley's ideal be produced and sustained outside a monastery, and without the help of men more skilled in formulating religious aims and applying them as a spiritual directorate than Wesley and his preachers proved to be? In the last resort, what kind of holiness, how complete a holiness, can emerge on the basis of traditional Protestant theology, committed also to a holiness open to all and in the world, even if (at its best) not of the world?

This survey of Catholic and Protestant approaches, with some of their historical developments in response to change, has been carried well into the 18th century. In the main we have concentrated on the internal problems encountered by these forms of Christianity which in themselves, particularly for Protestantism, created major stresses and conflicts. We have not stressed the more external secular pressures of a social and intellectual kind which in more recent times have come to bulk even larger in Christian eyes as a major source of religious difficulty. One type of intellectual pressure has been touched on, mainly with reference to Catholicism, in what is referred to loosely as the Enlightenment; but in fact the most drastic religious effects of this were more conspicuous in Protestant countries, and some of the basic problems raised then have continued to the present day. The difficulties of Protestantism so far discussed would probably have arisen in any social and intellectual situation; and to a considerable extent the development of both problems and attempted solutions could be seen within a traditional context both socially and intellectually. But the intellectual changes which culminated in the Enlightenment began to be evident and to affect religion in important ways from the end of the 17th century and indeed before. Then social and economic changes characterized as the 'Industrial Revolution' emerged from the end of the 18th century. It is these two series of changes which together have altered the condition of men and of their religion in ways which it has been thought convenient to analyse together in the next chapter.

4. The Historical Setting and Development of Modern Spirituality

A. Changes in Church and Society

1. *Social and Political*

Until the later years of the 18th century English society was still in many respects a relatively stable, rural, settled society, in which religion had an accepted and recognized place.[1] The existing Anglican established Church for all its admitted faults could still claim to be appropriate for the average religious life of this kind of world: a clerical gentleman in every parish, living on tithes (which in turn depended on landed property), responsible for the souls (and to a considerable extent the minds and bodies) of the inhabitants. Such a settled order of religion rested on the assumptions of a general belief in the supernatural and in Christianity, and a general habit of churchgoing, in a society which would not change so rapidly and drastically as to escape the traditional social and religious discipline of the parish.

Even in the 18th century there were signs of indifference to religion or at least to the parish church brand of it (hence one reason for the success of Methodism in some quarters); there had been intellectual difficulties (see next section), which, however, seemed to have been glossed over for the time being, and it would be an exaggeration to imply that there had not been continuing social change. Nevertheless, the worst shocks to the system began to operate from the later years of the century and have operated with increasing rapidity ever since.

There was, in fact, a double revolution which has since gone on to alter profoundly the nature first of English and then of the rest of Western society and, in consequence, that society's religion.[2]

First: the Industrial Revolution from, say, the 1780s which eventually transformed the old, settled, in many respects still half rural, social order into a troubled, over-crowded, rapidly expanding, urban civilization. By 1851 just over half the English population was urbanized. The religious results of this, at one level at least, may in all probability be seen in the fact that at that time less than half the population attended church, perhaps only one in ten in some of the greatest towns.[3]

Second: a 'democratic' revolution which to a consider-able extent was influenced by industrialization, though also by the long-term effects of the French Revolution of 1789 and earlier attempts at reform. There was a decline in the rule of privileged minorities and institutions; there was the slow growth of more representative government in a more open society. The privileges of established Churches (like the Church of England) declined and so many aspects of life became less obviously subject to religious sanctions and the Church was less able to claim to affect all aspects of life. On the other hand the Church and its ministers were freer, if they wished, to act as a purely religious body dealing in more purely religious work – at the price of catering for a narrower sector of life among a narrower section of the population. Even these were more difficult to control in a slowly secularizing and more open society.

The social results of all this are complex, still at work, and still under analysis. One may nevertheless point with some assurance to two types of consequence which have followed for religion. First, on the more institutional side, one can see the breaking down of some of the old social and cultural divisions on which a good deal of denominationalism in religion really rested. (This is one cause of the decline of the English Free Churches and the rise of the Ecumenical Movement.) The ministry (as well as the Church at large) has been affected by the decline of its general social role and so of its status. The institutional nature of the Church is in question because the nature of society itself is changing (so many sociologists would say) from a closely-knit 'communal' pattern to a more loosely-knit crossing of 'associational' patterns. Second, on the more specifically religious side the social developments just described have helped to produce a situation which has been characterized as one of a growing 'secularization': the need for God in a crude interventionist sense becomes steadily less evident; the habit of worship and piety is broken by rapid social change.

The 20th century has seen the continuing effects of these processes over wider areas with progressively deeper effects. A high birth-rate and other social factors helped to mask or perhaps even in some measure to hinder the full effects of social change on the Churches during the 19th century; but thereafter these balancing factors weakened and it is clear that such observances as churchgoing and baptisms have decreased. One factor here has been the decline of active belief in Christianity which has extended from Victorian intellectuals and occasional working-class sceptics to a more pervasive atmosphere of doubt. A more pluralistic and permissive society has weakened the appeal of specifically Christian belief; and in so far as the Churches themselves have changed their teachings they do not seem to have won extra allegiance. The difficulties of the Churches in adapting their traditional structures based on an outmoded social structure have already been noticed. Equally important is the way in which thinking about society, the understanding of society and the manipulation of it has left the Churches and their beliefs standing, in apparent irrelevance, on the sidelines.

The significance of all this for Christian belief and practice will be indicated in general terms in the next section, and explored in more detail in the rest of the book.

2. Intellectual

At this point we may add what really amounts to a third 'revolution'. Although one may discern ways in which the developing intellectual crisis of Christianity was, during the 19th century and after, connected with the other revolutions referred to, and in any case produced similar results for religion at a more theological level, there are clear signs that important elements in the intellectual difficulties for traditional Christianity go back at least to the 17th century and emerge in radical 18th-century attacks on it.

Although the Renaissance and Reformation had in some important respects broken with past tradition, and it is possible to trace some of the roots of the 18th-century Enlightenment a good way back, it seems that its direct origins lie in the steady growth of experimental science and changes in intellectual outlook which together brought about changes in world-view which were open and widespread by the end of the 17th century. The resulting changes in fundamental religious outlook and so in spirituality may well seem in retrospect to be more drastic for religion than those stemming from the Reformation. The essential characteristic of this change lies in the upsetting of the traditional balance in all branches of Christianity between revelation and reason in favour of the latter. Earlier Christians had in the last resort regarded revelation as more important, more vital for human destiny, than reason; and as providing truths which reason could not. In some 18th-century circles reason comes to dominate all departments of knowledge including religion, and in sceptical circles comes to be used to criticize tradition. The problem for Christians was to justify the traditional Christian claim to have a 'revelation' over and above what may be known of God by 'natural' reason; and closely associated with this was the problem of finding a place and character for God in a universe which, as a result of scientific and philosophical developments, seemed to leave little or no place for his direct action. Although the question of the *existence* of God was rarely raised at this time it was, especially in terms of the very bare existence allowed him in contemporary assumptions, a very real question.

It is unnecessary to follow the course of the debate between the 'orthodox' and the 'Deists' in any detail. The essential debate was on these lines: all essential religious truth (it was assumed) must be susceptible of rational demonstration, even revelation needing at least to seem reasonable once it has been accepted as revelation. It was contended by the orthodox that, nevertheless, some special Christian revealed truths were known by revelation alone. From this position some moved to the assertion that revelation did not add anything to what was known by the light of natural reason, but that it merely made clear what could in principle, all things being equal, be known without revelation. If, however, the orthodox continued to hold to revelation, they did so on the basis of what was revealed by Christ as divinely inspired: his inspiration was guaranteed by his divine status, which in its turn depended on the evidence of prophecies about him and miracles done by him. These basic props of divinity were defended by the orthodox and attacked by some Deists in a constant controversy over the 'evidences' of Christianity. Although the Deists were reckoned to be defeated at the official level and English religion at least continued to consider itself rationally established, the spectre of materialism and its consequences had been raised. Three possible answers to this might be considered. God might be seen as at the beginning of the processes of the universe, creating the world but thereafter leaving it without interference: this was the virtual absentee, non-intervening God of the Deists. Or God could be seen as beginning the world but also (to preserve a 'presence' and to provide some essential elements in traditional theology) as interfering occasionally and miraculously in the process thereafter: this was the position of most of the 'orthodox' against the Deists. Finally, one could see God as somehow immanent in the whole world-process: a view which was to receive fresh life after the other views broke down, particularly in face of Darwinism in the 19th century, and which is implied in a number of subsequent attempts to reconcile, for example, religion and science.

These problems and possibilities, in however unsophisticated a form they are raised, must be regarded as fundamental to any kind of belief in God as it can be conceived in the light of scientific world-views which had already begun to develop from the 17th century, and had received increasing impetus in the 19th. Hence also the problems raised are involved in any attempt at a spirituality; for

49

spirituality rests, traditionally at least, on belief in an objective God: a God who in some sense must be supposed to 'intervene' in the world (or what is the point of intercessory if not also petitionary prayer?) and who must in any case be supposed to be open to 'communion' with men in their spiritual exercises. These issues, and the possibility of spirituality without this kind of belief in God, will be discussed in the last chapter. For the moment it is only necessary to point to the process of secularization which in the present context takes the shape of a growing sense of autonomy in men, with a corresponding exclusion of God seen as necessary for interpreting the workings of the universe and man.

As has already been hinted, the full implications of the new modes of thought were not seen for a long time, and in England in particular the basic belief in supernatural religion was preserved in a conservative form well into the 19th century and postponed the impact of more radical ideas (e.g. on the Bible and philosophy) which were developing in Germany. But one of the fundamental pressures to which modern spirituality is subject had now come into being and had come to stay, in the shape of the concepts of the autonomy of the universe and of man, and the denial of supernaturalism. This was renewed, reinforced and extended in the 19th century and after.[4] Historical and literary studies developed and were applied to the Bible; further scientific studies – notably the Darwinian line – raised fundamental questions about the world, humanity and God; and in general the 'scientific' approach spread to ever wider fields, including the social sciences. This meant that in *every* field of investigation and in more and more corners of each field, the assumption of secular and rational, non-supernaturalist explanation seemed to hold good. In addition, certain major theorists in the various fields were prepared to advance theories which suggested that either their own field of thought provided a total explanation of human behaviour or that a number of 'natural' explanations in various fields did so: in both cases 'God' and the supernatural were seen as unnecessary or positively untrue hypotheses.

One may take examples almost at random. Feuerbach, for example, contended that 'God' is not an objective transcendent power, as had been assumed even by Deists, but a projection of men's thoughts and desires. In that sense there is a basis of 'reality' in him: men are indeed talking about *something*, but what they are talking about is in fact a version of themselves – humanity's aspirations deified. The essential point is that God is a human creation; he has no independent existence. To take an example of the effects of this on spirituality: 'Prayer is the self-division of man into two beings – a dialogue of man with himself, with his heart.' If prayer, as Schleiermacher had believed, expresses 'dependence' it is 'that of man on his own heart, on his own feelings'.[5] Although, as the opening pages of *The Essence of Christianity* demonstrate with devastating clarity, Feuerbach's views were argued from large metaphysical assumptions and not on the basis of empirical evidence, they well express the implications of the declining belief in the supernatural; and we shall return to this again in looking at some contemporary views of God and prayer which are in essence very similar.

Freud's theories about religion are also in part a product of metaphysical assumptions and not simply (as they purport to be) deductions from the empirical findings of his psychological investigations. The idea that God is simply a projection of an idealized and sublimated image of the human father not only resembles Feuerbach's view in principle, but is readily criticizable if it claims to be based on empirical or historical evidence.[6] The real significance of Freud for religion lies in other directions. He throws light on the perversion of religion; his work on psychology cannot be ignored by anyone, for example, Schleiermacher, who attempts to base authority in religion on 'religious experience'; and, more positively, as has already been remarked, for those concerned with spirituality he opens a door to the possibility of dealing more realistically with motivation.

Then there is Darwinism. In its properly biological form this was a threat in itself to the literal historicity of Genesis, to the traditional theology of the Fall and Original Sin, to the 'spiritual' nature of man, and to the idea in general of an 'intervening' God. Darwin himself lost belief in God as a result of his own theories.[7] Men like Huxley, deeply concerned about humanity and morality, found it difficult to avoid materialistic implications for thought and morality. Yet the broad concept of 'evolution' (which it would have been less misleading to call 'development' in the non-biological field) was used in a variety of ways before and after Darwin, not merely to do justice to historical change and to support theories of progress, but also to defend as well as to attack religion. Other Darwinian concepts like the 'survival of the fittest', itself originally borrowed from social observation, were reapplied to social studies and theories, in the shape of evolutionary concepts of society.[8]

This brings us above all to Karl Marx and his successors. Marx criticized Feuerbach for speaking only in terms of 'theoretical' rather than 'practical-critical' activity. 'Feuerbach starts out from the fact of religious self-alienation, the duplication of the world into a religious, imaginary world and a real one. His work consists in the dissolution of the religious world into its secular basis.' But this leaves the chief work still to be done. 'Once the earthly family is discovered to be the secret of the holy family, the former must then itself be criticized in theory and revolutionized in practice.' Feuerbach 'does not see that the "religious senti- ment" is itself a *social product*, and that the abstract indivi- dual whom he analyses belongs in reality to a particular form of society'.[9] The force of Marx's point of view (despite the endless criticisms of it) remains enormous in that it points to a completely secular explanation of society. A recent Marxist use of some of Bonhoeffer's 'religionless Christianity' ideas shows how easily radical Christianity in some forms merges into more explicitly and exclusively secular attitudes. Hanfried Müller sees 'religionless Chris- tianity' as a final vindication of man against the religious world-view of the West so that the Christian can take up a secular *Weltanschauung* which requires neither a formal concept of God nor an institutional Church for its completion. In this Godless world the 'comrade' replaces the neighbour as the bearer of the Word, and communion is mani- fested in Communist society. This is to express Christ's suffering lordship over the whole of society without the elect community of the church.[10]

Thus, in the social and physical sciences what emerges is a world seen in terms of self-regulating mechanisms. It has been pointed out[11] that later scientific and social thinking has tended to destroy these confident 'syntheses' of the 19th century: the impression becomes rather one of disorienta- tion and dislocation so far as comprehensive mechanistic world-views based on a single concept in the manner of the last century are concerned. 'Relativism' replaces 'evolution' as a popularized version of a scientific concept expanded to apply beyond its proper sphere. A greater stress than before has sometimes been laid on the unconscious, mass, irrational and non-mechanical elements both in personality and in society. In this situation philosophical and religious theories have been devised to take advantage of man's disorientation, sometimes utilizing the non-mechanistic elements in life and outlook. But where mystery has once again been felt to be present, mysticism has not automatically been evoked.[12] In fact, even where a greater stress is laid on the less mechanistic and rational sides of life, this is done with a view to the improvement of rational understanding and so rational manipulation and control. The understanding and action which follow are then worked out from an essentially secular point of view and continue to assume the irrelevance, if not the non-existence of the 'intervening' God.

3. Society, Thought and Spirituality

What has been described in the last two sections of this chapter adds up to a profound change in Western European sensibility, due to interlocking social and intellectual factors. Until the 19th century (and of course in some circles up to the present, but here we are talking about long-term and growing trends) belief in God was almost universal; and belief in an intervening God was common. By that time, it is true, the visible and tangible signs of his presence and the means of its expression were beginning to be limited in the Church as well as in the world. Religion in the 18th century – and some of these characteristics persisted long after – was by no means purely rationalistic, far less merely materialistic, as we have seen. The religion preached by Tillotson, whose spirit did indeed brood over a great deal of English religion in this period, was a partial but not total reduction of religion to morality; with the addition of certain dogmas and sacramental practices, a liturgy, and the ultimate sanctions of heaven and hell. This is really a transitional stage from an older kind of supernaturalist religion to a newer kind of rational religious morality, of the type theoretically laid out with great logical force by Kant.[13]

The persistence of a relatively settled social order was important in preserving the ritual habit of worship in a good many areas, especially in the countryside and small towns, and this was not everywhere and at once shattered by industrial change. There could, moreover, in a situation of changing social classes, be good reasons for religious observance at the level of churchgoing appropriate to one's (new) social class in a situation where this symbolized class change and respectability. It is in the present century and in this country that the decline of this kind of conformity is more clearly seen.[14] Another illustration of the way in which social pressures could for a time stimulate as well as stultify religious practice is the tendency of the French aristocracy, which had often been indifferent or sceptical towards religion in the 18th century, to return to the bulwark of religion after the Revolution had set on foot threats to all established social values.

The sober moralizing of 18th-century religion, and indeed its uniformly 'enlightened' character, can easily be exaggerated. Much can be said in favour of its attempts to curb and civilize passions which were often not far below the glossy surface beloved of writers on the age of elegance and Georgian calm.[15] There were, in any case, other types of religion present. The Evangelical Revival has been discussed separately elsewhere. That Revival recovered or intensified the old sense of God's reality for some in the personal drama of salvation and in the sense that even nature was under his control.[16] The same thing happened, in a different manner and in terms of a different theology and spirituality, well into the 19th century in the shape of the Oxford Movement in England and Catholic revivals elsewhere: a remarkable comeback though an imperfect one (see later). Beyond these circles a generalized, if often half-superstitious supernatural sense survived as long as the

55

majority of men, particularly in a rural setting, were so obviously a prey to unpredictable natural forces which could only be partially controlled: thus Providence could still be invoked and prayer of the crude petitionary and intercessory kind still be offered. But the scope and nature of the supernatural in these terms was bound to decline as technology advanced; and thus one major traditional motive for worship, deeply embedded in human nature or at least in human custom, declined.[17] This is one outstanding effect for spirituality of the general changes we have been describing. It has already been observed that the other major stimulus to worship at the popular level of social habit declined in effectiveness as a result of industrialization and urbanization, because the controls of rural and small-town life did not operate for immigrant and large-scale populations in huge cities.

Thus, in an industrial, urban, science-based society, the mystery departs from natural processes both in the natural and in the human world: harvest, birth, marriage and death – traditional points of connexion for the Church with the conventional religious observances of society. Habits of worship are broken in a mobile population. These are the things which affect conventional, mass religious observance of the kind most easily shown statistically. Religious observance beyond this minimum is rather the practice of the more earnest section of the churchgoing public. But they are subject to the same secularizing pressures and, in addition, to the pressures of the intellectual scepticism arising from reflection on God, the supernatural and religion, which have already been described. And, indeed, the longer these intellectual pressures go on, the more they are likely to affect the unconscious assumptions of the public at large. It is not a matter of the quibbles of a few intellectuals, as has already been pointed out; and it is in any case a mistake to assume than even the most casual and thoughtless occasional worshipper ignores the question of whether religion is in fact true and reasonable in what it claims and practises.

The Protestant position and Protestant spirituality has proved particularly vulnerable to all these pressures: it was stated at the beginning of this essay that this was one reason for paying most attention to the problems of Protestantism to illustrate modern spirituality. One might speculate on a number of questions here. How far has Protestantism in fact nurtured the world-view which has undermined its faith? Or how far is it rather that a situation which would have arisen anyway has affected Protestantism more quickly? If it has, is this really because change has occurred sooner and more rapidly in Protestant countries rather than in Catholic ones? Or is there something inherent in the Protestant form of Christianity which dooms it to be a degenerating heresy?[18] It may be suggested that the Protestant position is peculiarly vulnerable to the kind of changes we have been describing, though it is becoming increasingly evident that Catholicism is now being affected as well; and it is perhaps also true that with the exception of explicitly fundamentalist groups and sects, the decline in Protestant strength tends to be in inverse proportion to the height of its churchmanship and approximation to Catholic norms. There are many reasons for any truth there is in these generalizations, but a few points may be made in explanation. The Protestant symbolic and sacramental sources of piety were always (we have said) much sparser and less compelling to the average worshipper than are those of the Catholic, particularly when the religious experience on which Protestantism tends to depend has worn thin or become conventional. The Protestant staples of Bible reading and prayer have been particularly vulnerable to the intellectual developments of recent times, as we have seen;

57

and with these undermined, the more emotional and physical channels open to the Catholic are largely lacking. The territories where Protestants have been strongest have been those most quickly industrialized; and Protestantism has historically been the kind of religion most open to social and intellectual changes and to their sceptical implications. It must be added that Catholicism is also in its practices wide open to those social and intellectual changes which we have seen as tending to undermine religion as a ritual and habit linked with the mysteries of nature. In this connexion it is to be observed that industrialization of traditionally Catholic countries may be expected to be injurious to popular religious observance, as has already been the case in Western Europe.

Two final observations should be added. One is that this chapter has been a description of trends, and trends to change: one must not overlook the power of tradition and of churchgoing; or the effects of religious renewal of various kinds; or the attempts of Christianity to rethink its intellectual basis. All these may have helped to slow down the process of secularization or at least to modify its results for religion. (Some of them will be considered in the rest of this book.) But all such traditions and efforts have had to face the steady dissolution of the old certainties and, above all, of the old accepted (if abused) sense of the supernatural. And this, we repeat, seems basic to any system of worship which is more than auto-suggestion.

The other observation, which is equally important for our subject and is of a more positive and hopeful nature, is to state quite firmly that while the present writer takes the view that 'secularization' is a fact which cannot be explained away,[19] it is a fact which should in many respects be welcomed and not (as is still commonly the case with churchmen and theologians) deplored. The welcome is deserved for good secular reasons but also for religious ones. In a sentence: it can be seen as a process through which many of the props – social, intellectual, even 'religious' – on which the Churches and Christianity have relied during much of their history have been knocked away. The loss of many of these supports does not necessarily entail the disappearance of Christianity: it may mean its liberation. At all events the more modest claim may be made, which we hope to substantiate at the end, that there is here an opportunity (indeed a necessity) for the development of a rational and realistic spirituality.

In the remainder of this chapter we shall give some examples of how Catholic and Protestant traditions in spirituality have attempted to meet the changes in society and religion which have been described so far.

B. The Christian Response

1. Catholicism

(a) Religious Thinking and Spirituality

As was made clear at the start, our chief concentration is to be on Protestant problems, and consequently only a very brief sketch of a few outstanding developments on the Catholic side will be attempted here. I shall concentrate on the signs of change and adaptation and the significance these have in relation to the Catholic tradition of piety; and for this purpose it will be convenient to draw a good deal of the illustrative material from France.

In so far as Catholicism, in a more extreme fashion and for a longer period than Protestantism, has regarded itself as the sole true form of Christianity and, as such, entitled to an established if not in some respects dominant position in the social order, the shock of modern developments towards a pluralist society has been correspondingly great, with extensive intellectual consequences. Until the French Revolution it had normally been taken for granted that some positive connexion between Church and State was appropriate, and normally in the shape of an established Church with an extensive stake in society. The 19th-century trend was towards the dissolution of this concept: the replacing of church-controlled by secular institutions (for example, in education), and the toleration of a variety of denominations on a basis of more or less equal competition. The pace and extent of the change varied. The French Church was not finally separated from the State until 1905; the establishment of the English section of the Anglican Church still survives, though the Irish and Welsh establishments have not. In the same way the Papacy lost all but a final scrap of secular territory, and its temporal claims had consequently to be curtailed greatly in comparison with its medieval assertions, despite the fears of some statesmen in 1870. The growth of Ultramontanism in the 19th century may be seen partly as a spiritual compensation for the loss of more temporal claims on society, and partly as an attempt to reaffirm a religious basis for existence in face of growing claims to a secular control and a secular basis for all areas of life.[20] But the long series of condemnations of non-monarchical regimes, of control of church education, and of 'socialist' attitudes to society have manifestly been modified in the direction of a qualified acceptance of ideas which clearly emanate from the 'world' and not from the 'church'. The prophecies of Lamennais and the Liberal Catholics of the 19th century have tended to come true.[21]

Social change has been equally if not more potent. Take the French example. The French Revolution marked a break in church influence at the level of property and of the social and religious hold of the Church on common life. Recovery was incomplete and further hindered by industrialization. The more virulent and permanent anti-clerical and anti-religious strain in French life after the Revolution accentuated the socially based division between the Church and the working classes in particular. The efforts of French sociologists of religion have made this picture more specific than elsewhere and the notion of 'dechristianized' areas and 'France pagan' has been popularized. [22] These developments were to some degree obscured or hindered both by the partial revulsion of the aristocracy and later of the middle classes from the horrors of the Revolution back to religion as part of the old order of life; and this was reinforced by the persistence of the conservative attachment of the rural peasantry to the old religious order based on the ritual and symbolic links between religious practice and an agricultural society. After the restoration of the monarchy in 1815 there were Catholic *missions* designed to renew religious practice by a kind of 'revivalism' based on the renewal of baptismal vows, repentance and confession using the emotional resources of preaching and sacramental symbolism. Such efforts were in a measure successful and the reason seems to be that the secularization of society and feeling had not proceeded so far as to render the symbolism involved ineffective; and the reason for this was, in all probability, that neither had the social change due to industrialization yet proceeded very far.

In the present century such methods are unlikely to succeed, and it is in the light both of a deeper secularization and of changing attitudes towards it in some sections of Catholicism that one should view more recent French attempts at rechristianization. Here one thinks of the Mission de France and the Worker Priests.[23] The extent of the success or failure of these efforts, and the reaction of the hierarchy to them, are significant in several respects. There is the recognition by those involved of the extent to which

61

the Church's message and life are affected by its general social setting and consequently a sense that the Church's 'presence' in society and the way in which it presents its message must be aligned with existing social realities. They did make a serious attempt to break away from traditional ecclesiastical institutions and methods and to make a first-hand contact with areas of society which had long lacked any such religious contact. This created difficulties and tensions of various kinds: the old parish structure and congregation did not combine easily with the new methods and organization; the worker priests were in danger of ceasing to be under discipline, ceasing to observe liturgical and devotional rhythms, becoming absorbed in secular life. They became involved in trade unions and in politics; this not only created problems with more conservative church-men but meant that they were virtually ceasing to be priests and becoming compromised by Communism. The results well illustrate the problems of the relationship of Church and world, priests and laity, traditional spirituality and life in society, dramatized and heightened because it was priests who were involved in 'lay' life. The ending of the original experiment and its restarting in a modified form seems on the face of it to amount to a large measure of withdrawal from the original attempt at total involvement in working-class society. But it has been suggested (24) that the failure was really theological. Priests had learned in their seminaries to despise theology; they had believed in the effectiveness of non-intellectual evangelism. When they encountered real Marxists they had no serious theological defences: their anti-Communism had never been truly intellectual and many of them, trying to cope with and indeed to adopt the social attitudes of Communism, drifted into positions which were theologically untenable. It should be added that recent developments in some Roman Catholic quarters indicate a greater appreciation and more profound understanding of Marxist positions and a desire to engage in dialogue: for example, the 'Slant' group in this country. But this brings us naturally to complete this brief survey with a glance at theological changes.

The theological reaction of Catholicism to the implications of a secular world-view in the terms outlined earlier in this chapter seemed initially to be negative and disappointing. Conservative 'romantic' Catholics after the Revolution – men like Chateaubriand, De Maistre and De Bonald – attributed all evils to the Revolution and called for a return to the past and to authority: the authority of tradition, of the Church, of the Papacy, of 'legitimate' monarchy. The celebrated 'citadel' mentality of Pius IX, which only too faithfully represented the attitude of many of his Catholic contemporaries, seemed to point the same way: to the rejection of all reform, change, and 'modern' thought as potentially ruinous to the claims of Christ and his Church. It has been contended that this was necessary to stem the erosions of sheer unbelief which often lurked behind apparently attractive programmes of modernization; and that once Pius had (as in the Syllabus of Errors) laid down Catholic principle, it was safe (as under his successor Leo XIII) to make tactical and more than tactical concessions to a sound adjustment to changed conditions. But the impression of hostility to the modern world persisted. One popular example may be illuminating. In the preface to a book on *The Virgin Mary in the Nineteenth Century* (a collection of Mariological miracles and visions) the issues are made explicit. The 19th century has been an age of criticism and disbelief in the supernatural; Marian phenomena were, however, miraculous evidences of the existence of the supernatural to a doubting world.[25] One might say that these phenomena and the devotions associated with them fulfilled the same function for many Catholics' faith and piety as the phenomena of certain types of revivalism for some sections of Protestantism, in the checking of unbelief. Yet in both cases the remedy in the long run might prove to make belief and piety more and not less difficult.

However, other approaches made their appearance: attempts at a modern apologetic, at the modification or reinterpretation of traditional belief, so as to bring the essentials of Catholicism into line with modern knowledge while avoiding the latter's more sceptical implications. Here a certain line runs from Möhler and then Döllinger to Newman and finally the Modernists of the turn of the present century. This is not to say that the line is one of connexion and influence or even of logical consequence. Yet the overall aim has features in common. The key concept in all these cases is the recognition and acceptance of change and in some sense of 'development' in theology; and the crucial questions are always these: What areas in Catholic thought are subject to change, and in what sense? How far does change go and what is the relationship between the unchanging and the changing? Different answers to these questions implied very different theologies and the difference between orthodoxy and heresy.[26]

Viewed from a mid-20th-century perspective in which much that was once thought immutable has been accepted as mutable, one may make two comments. One is that the idea of development in doctrine which once was widely rejected (as seems implied by the approach of Pius IX) and nearly ruined Newman, has clearly now been accepted. But the idea is interpreted (as in Newman) as development in the sense partly of making explicit, partly of reinterpretation, of what always has been true and was always in the faith of the Church, given in the original revelation. Actual error in the past, or change in the present, in fundamentals, does not seem admissible. Moreover, care is taken not to subject Catholic thought to the claims of other systems; this was felt to be the fundamental error of the Modernists[27] who moreover seem at times to think in terms of a development or change in the original given essence of Catholicism and not merely of its elucidation. They also – unlike Newman, who used 'development' to justify essentially conservative theological positions and the miracles of popular piety – tended to set the natural and the supernatural in separate and even mutually contradictory categories.[28] This is the very problem, however, which remains fundamental for any modern Christian; just as behind this lies the equally fundamental problem of authority.

In the present century we have seen Catholic thinking in all fields overcoming selectively the earlier, too enthusiastic, reception or rejection of modern thought. 'Development' helps in distinguishing between, so to speak, the substance and accidents of Catholic thought. Distinctions between doctrinaire anti-Christian versions of various modes of thought and acceptable features in the same systems have enabled Catholic *rapprochements* with a wide range of non-Catholic thought. Thus the condemnation of Modernism has been followed in due course by the recognition of, for instance, biblical criticism, evolution, social doctrines. The question is really how far this acceptance can go – how far it really *does* go – without the final product either ceasing to be connected with a Catholic basis or else failing to accept the real force of ideas coming from a non-Catholic setting. On the whole, one feels that liberal Protestantism has been more radically open to an acceptance of fresh ideas, has felt less bound to 'reconcile' traditional doctrines to such ideas and has dared rather to reconcile tradition to modernity, while recognizing the risks involved. So often one feels, after reading a liberal, even apparently radical, Catholic writer – a Teilhard de Chardin, Wicker, Küng – that at the end one is presented with a continued acceptance of the traditional philosophy of 'being'; the Church as the basis of salvation; Church (including Papal) authority, however modified, as the basis of all religious authority; liturgy and sacraments (however modernized) as the basis of worship; and traditional asceticism as the basis of spirituality. Protestant or secular thought is used but not allowed to lead to *fundamental* changes of view such as their logic may really require.[29] Thus, as stated, one continually returns to fundamental questions of authority.[30]

(b) The Theory and Practice of Spirituality

An indication of the kind of effect the developments so far described could have on a sensitive if rather vague 'Liberal' Catholic in the early 19th century may be seen in Lacordaire, for whom perennial personal difficulties achieved a new urgency in contemporary conditions. 'One of the trials of being a monk', he said, 'is to live with men you have not chosen, most of whom arouse no natural sympathy within you; so that you are forced on to terms of intimacy without that touch of affection which reconciles and endears it to your soul.' The lack of sense of purpose in the monastic life is interesting; so is the legacy of Rousseau, and the human rather than divine aim implied. He prefers the (Dominican) friars to monasticism for the modern world and again gives a secular reason for their value as the 'remedy for the scourge of individualism in voluntary societies based on labour and religion'.[31]

Much of 19th-century piety was directed towards a revival of traditional patterns (as in the case of the *missions* in France referred to earlier). Liturgy also did not alter in its essential aims and practice: the Abbé Guéranger, often seen as in some sense a pioneer of the Liturgical Movement, was rather what one might call a Gothic Revivalist in a liturgical sense.[32] In the setting of English Roman Catholicism it is instructive to notice the often mentioned contrast between the old-fashioned, comparatively sober, piety of the native tradition being challenged by the injection of Italianate piety in some of the Anglican converts like Faber, whose London Oratory was itself in contrast with Newman's at Birmingham. Yet Newman was here, as in theology, really a conservative, adopting traditional practices, as he accepted ecclesiastical miracles, by a deliberate act of faith.

It is not until the present century that one finds real doubts about tradition creeping in, which find expression in the spiritual problems of the worker priests; the devising of orders and rules for a more 'in-worldly' situation; the growth of the Liturgical Movement and its social consciousness; and the piety 'in the world' and indeed 'of the world' implied in Teilhard and, say, Michel Quoist.

It would seem that Catholic, like other piety tends to assume a 'religious sense' in man; this is implied in the Thomist approach to theology and in much Catholic reform (including the reform of worship). Renew worship in acceptable forms and all will be well. Men are bound to respond once the obstacles of archaism are removed. We have, however, earlier in this book raised the question whether these assumptions will do. There are in fact signs in some recent Roman Catholic writing of fairly fundamental reappraisals of the modern situation influenced by similar considerations to those which have affected radical Protestants. This is to some extent true of (for example) Brian Wicker's *Culture and Society* though it was suggested above that the presuppositions to which he returns are really not unlike those of more traditional Catholicism; corporateness and liturgy solve all the problems in the end. Or there is Robert Adolfs's *The Grave of God*[33] : he sees the fault of the Church as its association with temporal power and appears to believe that a drastic revision of its structure aligned to the 'associational' patterns of modern society will solve its problems. Or there are the less traditionalist preoccupations and experiments of Dutch Catholicism.[34]

A more fundamental question is raised by Claude Geffré.[35] He rightly rejects the view of those who see the only hope of the recovery of Christianity in the reversal of 'desacralization'. Geffré sees this as not only impossible but undesirable, for this very process towards a 'controllable' universe and the destruction of the old mysteries on which religion once built leads, he thinks, to questions of 'meaning' and so back to religion. One feels all the same that he still believes in a religious 'sense' and in rather traditional (for example, liturgical) means to evoke and satisfy it. It is unusual, indeed, to find any questioning of the enormous expectations built on liturgy.[36]

An important element in all serious Roman Catholic reassessments of spirituality would seem to be a fresh look at the concepts and relationships of 'church' and 'world', 'clergy' and 'laity', and the implications these have for the aims of Catholic spirituality and the situations in which it may be practised. Consider, for example, the religious orders. As we have seen, these have varied from the totally enclosed to those immersed in activities in the world. Correspondingly, there is a variety of appropriate rules. Recent religious orders have experimented further – the inspiration of Charles de Foucauld comes to mind.[37] But behind these efforts still lurk the old problems: the notion of the primary relationship to God persists in a way it has not usually done in modern Protestantism, but the implementation of this has persistently implied a view of the 'two standards'. The

68

pressure for an 'in-worldly' piety is there, but is limited not merely by traditional patterns of devotion, but even more by the sense that some kind of (celibate) community or at least rule of life is necessary, and this includes at least a community base, a house really abstracted from society even though set in the midst of it, and so on. (The question will be raised in the last chapter whether this kind of minimal discipline can in fact be avoided if an organized body is not to break down.)

More promising in this respect is the approach to piety implied in and indeed practised by the worker priests. Here at least was an attempt to face the problem inherent in a Protestant spirituality, a combination of 'the idea of forsaking the world with the deliberate embracing of it in its most typical form of industrial work',[38] marred, however, by celibacy, which understandably became a problem for some of the priests. But the pull towards an 'in-worldly' piety continues to show itself in contemporary Catholicism: for example, Michel Quoist's *Prayers of Life*[39] attempt to get away from the traditional piety of making 'worldly' material 'sacred' and at least reflect the actual experiences of a man in one kind of 'worldly' situation. More fundamentally, one can see in the theology of Teilhard an attempt to take the evolutionary process as divine, and in his *Mass on the World* express this in terms of an actual spiritual exercise.[40]

This piety, 'in the world' yet sanctifying it and linking it with the Church, is also one major feature of the Liturgical Movement in Catholicism and in Anglicanism which has been one of the most comprehensive expressions of Catholic reform and renewal in recent times and indeed includes more than its name suggests.[41] One can, of course, appreciate the criticism (which is quite often justified) that this is mere antiquarianism, propping up the shaky status of the clergy.

For Catholicism at least it has a wider usefulness; one might almost regard it as a kind of Trojan horse to which this generation of Catholic modernizers has resorted in order to make respectable a number of biblical, doctrinal and social ideas which had come to grief prematurely as a result of the reign of terror following the Modernist fiasco. The results range from the modest to the radical, but they are at the least a dose of many of the things for which Protestants (and some Catholics) pleaded at the Reformation; and often more than this. The central theme has been the Eucharist as central to public and private piety; a Eucharist for the laity; a Eucharist seen as the symbol and vehicle of taking the life of the world into the Christian community and the Christian community empowered to go out into the life of the world. The question is – and this will be raised again for Protestantism and in the last chapter – whether this symbolism is sufficiently in tune with contemporary society's psychology; whether certain theological questions are not too readily glossed over, if the central act of the Liturgy is used to carry the enormous burden of the religious, social and evangelistic meaning which is claimed for it.

2. *Protestantism*

(a) Religious Thinking and Spirituality

While acknowledging the continuance of more traditional modes of thought and the spirituality associated with them, we shall here be concerned mainly with those who have in various degrees and various ways attempted to accept the reality of drastic problems for religion in modern times and to devise theoretical solutions for them. We shall be taking particular note of the problems and solutions considered in direct relation to certain aspects of spirituality; but the more practical solutions attempted will be reserved for section (*b*) below, which will also include a consideration of some more conservative approaches.

The underlying problem, as has already been hinted more than once, has become one of belief in God – or at least of articulating and justifying such a belief (the two are not quite the same). From another point of view the problem might be described as that of the basis of 'authority' in religion. Once these things become problematical, the whole business of constructing a 'spirituality' in anything like the traditional sense of communion with God becomes problematical as well. The problem, so far as it centres on belief in God, has been clearly posed in this manner: the 'God of classical Protestantism [and the essence of the problem ought really to hold good for Catholicism as well] presented His people with an objective revelation of Himself in Christ and in the Scriptures; theologically, even faith in God was stirred up by God Himself in the Holy Spirit and so was objectively given: the subjective element in revelation so to speak was God Himself taking over our human faculties'.[42] But for those who are commonly termed Liberal Protestants in the 19th century and after (that is, those feeling the full impact of modern thought and endeavouring to come to terms with it) 'the situation is more difficult to define'. They 'became steadily more nervous about asserting what might be called the objective content of the doctrine of God; more concerned to argue that it is almost impossible to speak with *certainty* of objective knowledge of God'. Such a Protestant 'felt, what classical Protestants did not feel, that the materials for a doctrine of God had been drastically reduced in the course of the 19th century'. The same writer suggests that the sources of this 'reduction' included: the moral criticism of traditional ideas of the plan of salvation (e.g. penal substitution, eternal punishment),[43] the effects of science on ideas of miracle and

Providence and divine intervention in general; biblical criticism (which did not in the end produce the expected clear new version of religion); and philosophical criticism (which seemed to question the very possibility of a metaphysic and so removed the usual foundation for a doctrine of God).

One may add once again that social pressures of the kind already described played their part in reducing the consciousness of God and the supernatural. As an early and unusually clear example of what pressures of this kind could lead to, and their logical effects on spirituality, we may take one characteristic writing of Kant, *Religion within the Limits of Reason Alone*[44]: for this writing (and Kant's whole position) not only shows the true meaning of the Enlightenment for the future of belief and piety, but also points forward to the kind of solutions which might in future be attempted.

Kant saw clearly that one could no longer base religion either on the old, externally imposed, revelation justified by miracles, etc.; or on some system of purely speculative reason. The only world we know directly is the physical world apprehended by our finite faculties of sense and reason; this is the 'phenomenal' world of order and causality whose laws can be understood and rule out miracle. The 'noumenal' world of ultimate reality which is assumed to lie behind this cannot so be known, and hence the traditional 'proofs' of God's existence turn out to be impossible. The only remaining channel to knowledge of God – the status of this as a 'proof' is not our concern here – is to ground religious faith on our inmost moral consciousness: the celebrated 'categorical imperative'. To do this admittedly seems to reduce religion to morality and Kant's version of 'religion' is commonly regarded as defective for this and other reasons. It has been pointed out[45] that it is purely individual and rationalistic and anthropocentric; it misses out large areas of religious experience as commonly understood, for example, the varieties of communion with God represented by the varieties of historic spirituality. In contrast with Schleiermacher (see below), Kant does not recognize a distinctive 'religious' experience at all. Nevertheless it may be contended that he represents very acutely and forcefully the religious dilemma not only of his own but also of succeeding times, that the direction in which he looked for a solution may in principle be the only plausible one, and that in particular the conclusions he drew for the actual practice of spirituality have a lasting significance.

This may be seen from his 'General Observations' at the end of *Religion within the Limits of Reason Alone*. The most we may assume about supernatural moral aid, he says, is that grace will effect in us what nature cannot, if we use our natural powers to the full; and this divine aid 'aims at nothing but our morality'. True moral service of God consists 'solely in the disposition of obedience to all true duties as divine commands, not in actions directed exclusively to God', which only lead to self-deception and so hinder morality. What about the usual visible means of grace? They are necessary to picture to us our duty in the service of God, yet dangerous as risking the illusion that they are in themselves the service of God.

Kant then sees the true (moral) service of God as consisting in four observances of duty which have become associated with four rites: the rites are simply useful means for securing our attention to the duties. Thus *private prayer* establishes the morally good in ourselves and awakens the disposition of goodness in the heart. *Churchgoing* spreads goodness abroad through a public assembly to express and share religious doctrines, wishes and dispositions. *Baptism* represents the propagation of goodness in posterity through the reception of new members in the fellowship of faith as a duty, and their instruction in goodness. *Communion* is the maintenance of this fellowship through a repeated public formality making enduring the union of members in an ethical body.

This may seem a caricature of religion, yet it does follow from Kant's basic exposition of the difficulty in seeing God except in terms of a moral sense. He condemns as 'fetish-faith' 'the persuasion that what can produce no effect at all according to natural laws or to moral laws of reason, will yet, of itself, bring about what is wished for, if only we firmly believe' that it will do so and go through the right formalities. He condemns in fact as 'illusory faith' all that involves overstepping the bounds of our reason 'in the direction of the supernatural', i.e. miracles and means of grace in the traditional meaning of the term. Prayer, for example, as a 'stated wish' to God is impossible; but if it is only working upon oneself by means of the idea of God it is better anyway and valid even if no reality of God is attained. Similar attitudes are taken to the other 'means' mentioned in turn.

The history of 19th- and 20th-century thought, it may be suggested, tends to show in convincing detail the force of what was stated above about the factors which made it difficult to hold traditional views of God. It also tends to show the fundamental truth of Kant's insight that one must look to religious experience and in the end religious experience interpreted in moral terms. Perhaps, it may be suggested finally, the story also gives some reason for believing that the end-results for the practice, or at least the interpretation, of piety are not so very different from what Kant saw them as being. On all these counts, however, there was a prolonged struggle to escape the Kantian position in its full rigour.[46]

74

Despite the efforts of the Romantics the post-Enlightenment world remained obstinately 'disenchanted';[47] if, like Wordsworth, you reanimate nature, are you doing more than putting a significance into it from your own mind? and if so, then are you really reintroducing *God* at all?

Post-Kantian Liberal Protestantism remained preoccupied with the basic problem of how to establish a 'place' for God to exist and a channel through which he may operate in a natural and human world which seems (as a law-abiding, self-sufficient mechanism) to exclude either possibility, let alone the possibility of knowing God if he does exist and work. Schleiermacher therefore looked for a specifically 'religious' area of experience to be seen in a sense of 'absolute dependence'; if valid, this does better than Kant, for one is not then reduced to mere morality. One can then validate the existence of God and a spiritual life based on this. When he discusses prayer it is clear that he sees the essential difficulty: he discusses this and regeneration in the context of 'miracle' and asserts that 'It can never be necessary in the interest of religion so to interpret a fact that its dependence on God absolutely excludes its being conditioned by the system of Nature';[48] a 'special divine causality' is excluded. Any talk of 'spiritual influence' or a restriction of prayer to 'spiritual blessings' is subject to exactly the same problems as the cruder kind of prayer for physical miracles. Yet if one removes an objective God or an objective moral order, one is left only with self-consciousness, self-cultivation, or (what is really the same) the kind of 'projection' of the self implied by Feuerbach. Schleiermacher seems in the end to rely on the general postulate that there is an overall divine plan and whatever happens through prayer is a part of this and therefore the 'ordinary' chain of causality is not broken.

Ritschl's approach shows a similar problem. He too recognized the absolute dominance of law as revealed by science; while he looked for some valid sphere of reality and basis of knowledge for religion.[49] 'Religious knowledge moves in independent value-judgements, which relate to man's attitude to the world, and call forth feelings of pleasure or pain, in which man either enjoys the dominion over the world vouchsafed him by God, or feels grievously the lack of God's help to that end.'[50] He concentrates therefore on a description of religious attitudes as 'value-judgements' made in relation to Christ's historical moral personality which gives us knowledge of God of at least a practical and moral kind. The development of the religious life in accordance with this gives us a certain freedom or 'lordship', religiously speaking, over the world which remains, however, determined by scientific law. Prayer becomes a faith in God's overall providence and an instrument to strengthen faith, which puts it nearly in the place reserved for it by Kant.[51]

It will be seen that Providence in general and prayer in particular posed continual problems for those taking the world of ordinary causality seriously. Réville saw the development of science as shattering the idea of miracle, affecting the idea of God and also one's view of prayer if this meant getting divine intervention to fulfil one's wants and save one from danger.[52] But other Liberals, rather like Schleiermacher and Ritschl, saw prayer as one of the distinctive features of religion, and as the means by which divine indwelling can take place.[53]

There were really two elements in the religious approach of Ritschl and his school: First, there was an appeal to religious experience as a road to God independent of the closed system of the ordinary causal universe; this was expressed in his 'value-judgements'. Second, there was a confident reliance (despite the sceptical biblical criticism of men like Strauss and Baur) on a clearly discernible historical Jesus as a revelation of God's values. Both these elements were developed to the extreme in men like Harnack and Sabatier who also developed further the Ritschlian picture of the essential 'values' of Christianity as those of a still evolving human brotherliness. For the Liberal Protestant, then, there are, as Herrmann put it,[54] 'two objective facts': 'the historical fact of the Person of Jesus'; and the fact that 'we hear within ourselves the demand of the moral law'. On this basis a distinctive Christian position and a life of devotion orientated to it are possible. But subsequent developments in biblical criticism have raised the questions whether the 'historical Jesus' was of the character that had been supposed; whether, indeed, his character could be clearly established at all. One had therefore to fall back on the second 'objective fact'. But what was the character of this? Was it distinctively Christian? Was it a merely moral or also a religious sense? Did it in the last resort represent anything 'transcendent' at all?

An early English example of this may be seen in the development of Benjamin Jowett, who came to see that most of traditional theology might become untenable or meaningless; that immortality, for example, would become only 'the present consciousness of goodness and of God'. 'Yet the essence of religion may still be self-sacrifice, self-denial, a death unto life, having for its rule an absolute morality, a law of God and nature – a doctrine common to Plato and to the Gospel.'[55] This essentially Kantian position is also present in Matthew Arnold who, however, retained a much more specifically Christian shape for his religion. This was because although he saw 'religion' as in the main morality, it was 'morality touched by emotion', its specific content being modelled on the historic teaching of Christ.[56]

Since, for both men, religion is essentially a particular kind of moral life, the traditional preoccupations with dogmatic 'proofs' and definitions of the Trinity and the Person of Christ being abandoned, much depends on the means of inculcating this practice. Here again Jowett was the more radical in his disillusionment with the visible church structure and traditional means of piety;[57] Arnold's more conservative attitude to church worship raised, however, problems of how far one can use ritual in senses other than those it ostensibly implies.[58]

The basic Liberal search for a religious or at least moral sense, and the assumption that there is one, has continued in the present century: one may cite the distinguished examples of Bultmann and Tillich, whose positions are, admittedly, more subtle and less optimistic than those of their 19th-century predecessors. The increasing difficulties of the older kind of Liberal reliance on the Jesus of History, and the destruction of the cruder forms of optimism once current, have led modern Liberals to base their use of the biblical material about Jesus not so much on its problematic historical authority as on its conformity to what are felt to be the more fundamental needs and aspirations of human nature: for example, the Existentialist categories of 'being' in Bultmann and the 'ultimate concern' sensed in the depths of one's personality in Tillich.

The search for a religious 'space' for God and the question of how it would be recognized if it existed is raised in an essentially contemporary form by, for example, van Buren or the 'Death of God' theologians.[59] Van Buren attempts to take both linguistic philosophy and Christ seriously as a way to a 'secular Christology', and he recognizes the obvious question: Although historical Christianity has a 'historical, intentional, and ethical dimension, does it not include a great deal more? Where is the transcendent God of classical Christianity? Have we not reduced theology to ethics?' But he concludes that there cannot now be any 'more'. In all fields of thought the subject matter has now been reduced to the human, historical and empirical; and this is not to be regretted in theology either. We are to think out our existence 'in terms of man – specifically the man in whom God has said all that he has to say to men'.[60] The 'Death of God' school is up against the same kind of difficulties which are dealt with in more or less radical ways with more or less startling language. The end-product is similar to van Buren's: an attempt to define Christianity without a 'transcendent' and in terms of man, specifically Jesus. Van Buren, in the passage just cited, uses the term 'God' in what must be a metaphorical sense, or perhaps in the sense of Feuerbach; it is not God he is talking about at all in any intelligible sense of the word, but men's human ideals. This is made more explicit in the language of the 'death of God' – a highly paradoxical mode of speaking. But in place of God there is Jesus – and, again, Jesus apparently as a man. However, the man Jesus is in effect made God by being given that place by men, not on some ground of revelation or metaphysics but by being taken as having the authority of God for moral purposes. This could in fact be done on two different grounds: One would be by some sort of assertion about 'divinity' or revelation of the 'transcendent' but the general position of these theologians does not make such a ground secure. The other possibility is, in accordance with fashionable ethical theory of our time, to take a Christian standard of morality as a basis for action without any more ultimate validity. In this case, however, no question of God, or revelation, or absolute standards arises, nor is there any reason that can be given for choosing Jesus as a standard. And finally, when one comes to examine the moral positions which are taken on the contemporary content of Christianity one finds that they are usually conceived in terms of a social gospel which lacks the factor which distinguished the old 'Social Gospel' of the turn of this century.[61] That movement had, indeed, not merely made social application of Christianity but also enlarged its theological content in a social direction. However, while this older social gospel did represent a shift towards a more 'secular', 'this-worldly' form of Christianity, its ultimate theological basis was the Incarnation: no such basis is possible in the 'Death of God' school; Jesus is a man. And the absence of any transcendent reference does appear to be serious in practice as well as in theory, since the content of the new, entirely social 'gospel' turns out to be an endorsement of existing fashionable social and political attitudes which ought not to need justification on 'Christian' grounds, may well not be sufficiently critical of society on social grounds, and in any case fail totally to add up to a specifically Christian standpoint as distinguished from humane concern in general. Hence, once again, one has to ask 'Why bring Jesus into the question at all?' What we have left as a 'spirituality' is really social activity without reference beyond men but based on unexamined human ideals; and if, for example, prayer persists it can only be in terms of auto-suggestion or of orientation to a (human) ideal – which is a reduction beyond even Kant and Jowett.[62]

Faced with these appalling difficulties, Christians who have wanted to avoid the even greater difficulties of fundamentalism have sometimes tacitly evaded the intellectual difficulties of their faith in the present century by claiming a channel of revelation or assumed basis of certainty which in fact 'solves' the problems we have outlined by not raising them. A great deal of so-called 'Biblical Theology' is of this nature. It is implied that the exact patterns of biblical teaching can be authoritatively determined and that once this 'theology' is expounded it will somehow prove to be a sufficient basis for faith. Both assumptions are untenable: this particular attempt at an agreed biblical interpretation (which has, significantly, proved capable of attracting fundamentalists and Roman Catholics as well as more radical writers) does not produce complete agreement and if it did it would not make the agreed theology any more credible or intelligible for men in our world. Nor does it so much as raise the real question of how a revelation can take place in view of the factors we have been discussing. Reliance on 'the Church' which has become a feature of Protestantism in recent times may also fill only too readily the gaps left by the dissolution of earlier Protestant 'authorities'. In a more sophisticated sense the Church may be seen, as it was by the early Bonhoeffer,[63] as the 'space' in which God operates in this world: a tradition with a long history behind it but which is as subject to the criticisms we have rehearsed as any other alleged 'space'. The Church is no more capable than the Bible of being a special self-authenticating type of religious activity. Finally, one may mention the Liturgical Movement, which will be considered more at large in a moment. Here the point to notice is that it too may become a subtle means of evading fundamental problems: that is to say, it may make an implied claim to be an effective channel for religious experience leading to a recovery of belief in God (whereas, like biblical theology, it may well raise more questions than it answers); or it may become a way of behaving as if what the ritual implies were true without actually facing the question of whether, in terms of the theological problems we have raised, it really is.

A much more fundamental assault on the problems faced by Liberal Protestantism has been the theology of Karl Barth and those he has influenced, which has been neatly characterized as a 'positivism of revelation'.[64] Barth simply denies the whole basis on which the Liberal Protestant approach to the problems of belief was founded. For Barth the whole trend of 19th-century theology turns God into an object which it is assumed the mind of man can discern; in fact, it is impossible for men to apprehend God in this way, and, whatever they do think they apprehend, it is not really God. It does not appear that Barth ever really retracted this basic position; and, far from attempting to solve the problems of finding a 'space' for God, he really underlines the problem as inherently insoluble. Like linguistic sceptics he denies the possibility of human reason saying anything valid about God; from the standpoint of reason both God and religion are nonsense. But it seems impossible to avoid 'human' talk about God: what other talk can there be unless one has a self-authenticating and infallible revelation? But Barth is not a fundamentalist; and if one denies fundamentalism, then one has no other resource but a *human* interpretation of any alleged revelation. Barth claims for his own theology (if it is to be anything at all beyond an ordinary human utterance about religion) a discourse about God and religion from a standpoint independent of human fallibility. If to 'natural' theology is opposed an alleged theology of revelation based on an exposition of the Bible, all that *can* be produced is what any other human being can produce, a human interpretation of what God allegedly said.

In fact, Barth is not even true to his own project which should have produced in a certain sense a 'religionless Christianity' – Christianity divested of human corruptions. As Bonhoeffer pointed out,[65] Barth had produced a 'positivism of revelation' open to all the difficulties of any alleged revelation; and he was not even consistent at that. Even in his early *Christian Dogmatics* (1927) he implied that the Church provides a certain imperfect 'parable' of God in the world; and in his later *Church Dogmatics*[66] a still greater place as *necessary* for Christianity if only as a 'parable'. But if this 'parable', why not others? No sane theologian has ever claimed to have a perfect formula for God. Barth, it must be categorically stated, has led theology into a dead end.

Kierkegaard, though one of the inspirers of Barth in his early period, is essentially a more formidable figure. He faced the 'Liberal' problem of finding a 'space' for God by really denying that any merely intellectual approach is possible at all. For example, he took up Lessing's objections to the project of 'proving' religious truths from historical facts (which undermines one of the main Liberal positions).[67] Only by a decisive leap from objective thinking into subjective and personal faith, with the consciousness of sin as the drawing power, can one attain Christianity and 'contingent contemporaneity' with Christ. Kierkegaard's concern was, moreover, not to 'prove' Christianity but to make plain what real Christianity is as distinct both from other modes of knowledge and experience and from false versions of itself. And in this concern the overriding aim (as his practical treatises under his own name made clear) was to persuade men, if not to become Christians, at least to have a constant awareness of how far they were from being Christians. He saw the Christian category as the 'absolute relation to the Absolute': 'The task is to exercise the absolute relationship to the absolute *telos* [end], striving to reach the maximum of maintaining simultaneously a relationship to the absolute *telos* and to relative ends, ... by making the relationship to the absolute *telos* absolute, and the relationship to the relative ends relative.'[68] To maintain this requires 'forsaking the world' – but Kierkegaard warns against interpreting this in a monastic or outwardly ascetic sense. The monk was right in making the standard high but wrong in limiting it to a special group of people; Luther was right in making the same standard for all, but Protestantism has been wrong in lowering the standard for all. One should combine the absolute demand and absolute renunciation implied by the monastery with the demand that it should be for all and in the world, marked not by an outward asceticism but by a constant inner consciousness of the relationship with the absolute of God's demands, which in relation to one's ordinary intercourse with the world should be a perpetual stimulus to renouncing worldly standards.[69] In his final *Attack on Christendom* (reflected also in the 'Journals' of that time) Kierkegaard despaired of and attacked established 'Christendom' as a betrayal of real religion. All this, however pessimistic it may seem both about the knowledge of God and the practice of spirituality, does offer some clues for a modern spirituality which will be followed up later; and, more important, remains a standing and haunting challenge to anything less than the 'absolute' demands of God on the individual.

As a final example of the fundamental problems of a place for God and a spirituality to cope with the difficulty of finding one, we may cite the case of Bonhoeffer.[70] If there is one theme linking together the earlier and the fragmentary and enigmatic later thinking of Bonhoeffer it is perhaps that of finding a 'space' for God in the sense we have been discussing, though this became most explicit at the end of his career. His early *Act and Being* was in line with the Barthian reaction against the Liberal attempts to locate a religious consciousness and so (as Barth was to urge) to subject God to the human mind. More firmly than Barth, however, he saw the Church as the 'community of revelation': even Christ only exists as the Church. In the period of *The Cost of Discipleship* he continued this theme, being conscious of a 'boundary' between Christ and the world set by the world's rejection of Christ. Much in the style of

Kierkegaard[71] Bonhoeffer in speaking of 'costly grace' saw Christianity and a 'worldly' life as incompatible – the world has been made 'Christian' at the cost of making Christianity worldly in a bad sense. During the struggle with Nazism in the 'Confessing Church' Bonhoeffer seems to have come to narrow down the locus of the Christological revelation to that Church only. From the point of view we have been following, this seems open to all the objections both to Barthianism and to a reliance on the 'Church' to solve the problem of the presence of God.

In his last phase, as reflected in the *Letters*, Bonhoeffer increasingly saw that this was so, partly because of the problem of the relation of the world outside the church community to the Church and Christ; partly because of a better understanding of history and its significance; but above all by his understanding of the significance of Nazism. On this basis he seems to have come to doubt the validity of the assumption that men have a 'religious instinct' on which so many church and theological reform programmes depend: hence the famous talk about 'man come of age' and 'religionless Christianity'. In the *Letters* the old boundaries between 'Church' and 'world' disappear, and so do the ecclesiological preoccupations. What remains is an interest in the participation of the disciple in the transcendent being of Christ; a freedom 'from' the world does remain as in his original thinking but now it is seen as a participation in Christ's 'being for others'. It is important and often not noticed that this is an attempt at expressing a kind of 'transcendent'.

All this has considerable importance for any idea either of 'revelation' or of a 'space' for God; and for spirituality. For revelation, Bonhoeffer's fresh understanding of history – in fact a recognition of what the liberals of the 19th century and in particular Troeltsch as one of the latest representatives of that tradition had been doing[72] – led him to turn away altogether from the basic preoccupation from which his original ecclesiology had started, the attempt to locate an 'empirical-revelational' 'space' for Christ in the world. Troeltsch had thought that man was really a religious animal with a religious consciousness: this, we have suggested, is dubious and in any case 'secularized' men are no more likely to accept such a view of themselves than they are to accept ideas of revelation. Seeing this, Bonhoeffer also saw (like Barth and perhaps Kierkegaard at least in this) that 'revelation' and not 'religion' is the proper way to speak of the Word of God which violates the structure of the world. To express this, while yet being completely true to the knowledge of the world, Bonhoeffer uses three key phrases (which also imply an appropriate spirituality for the situation he discerned): a 'this-worldly transcendence'; a 'non-religious interpretation of biblical concepts'; and a 'sharing in the sufferings of God at the hands of a godless world'.

A 'this-worldly transcendence' is a rejection of the traditional doctrine of God and the replacing of it with an understanding of transcendence focused on the worldly humanity of Christ and the participation of disciples through him in the life of the mature world. 'Christ, the man for others' is the final formula: i.e., an encounter with the 'being of Christ for others' is the expression of transcendence for us – a 'this-worldly transcendence' but still a transcendence, since it challenges and does not merely endorse ordinary human concerns. The 'secret discipline' supports and witnesses to that hope and love which cannot be *stated* in terms of this world in and of itself – there is no analogy to it in this world, for this too is given in Christ.

A 'non-religious interpretation of biblical concepts' (i.e. 'religionless Christianity') points to the consequences for theology. In all this Bonhoeffer recognized a fundamental fact for the modern theological situation: that for an indefinite period it would not be possible to *say* much about theology, since the old theological material (for example, for a doctrine of God and salvation) and the old theological language fitted to it had almost vanished. One could only 'pray and live for others' (both activities doubtless raising large problems) and out of this fresh experiment in the quest for religious life and experience one might rediscover religious material and a language to fit it from which theology might again emerge.

Finally, 'sharing in the sufferings of God at the hands of a godless world' points to a view of discipleship which attempts a recovery of a worldly form of 'imitation of Christ' as the centre of a theology of revelation (this dependence of theology on spirituality as well as vice versa is particularly important for the present study). This involves a dialectical, lived relationship, which relates 'sharing in the sufferings of God' to the 'secret discipline': the former occurs by living a worldly life; the latter by refusing the world any ultimate claims on oneself. (Compare the view of Kierkegaard about the inner suffering while living in the world, which is the result of the inner and invisible sense of the absolute: the verbal echo of the Early Church phrase is really rather misleading when it is taken to imply that Bonhoeffer is preaching a return to traditional spirituality.) Once again, one is aware of a contrast with the school of thought which simply identifies Christianity with a programme of humane social activity.

For Christian thought and so also for spirituality, the problem of our time continues to be to find some 'place' for God which can be rationally justified without denying the world as revealed by the sciences (natural and social). The possibilities seem to be: (1) One may posit different spheres or levels of activity. This might mean (i) that by adhering to the existing mode of scientific explanation one

87

could posit a 'law-abiding' activity of God which in fact operates in whatever ways science currently describes. This 'immanentist' view of God has been one popular way of accepting, for example, evolution: unfortunately it involves an initial belief in God which is not required by the material in view; it therefore really belongs with the view discussed below as (2). Alternatively, one may propose God's activity as really 'law-abiding', since any divine 'interventions', such as those in fact involved in any kind of 'providence' or prayer, are really examples of operations according to 'laws' as yet undiscovered.[73] But this is to bring all events once again under 'natural' explanations in principle, and once again there is no reason to posit God. The same applies even more forcibly if only the (diminishing) 'gaps' in the explicable world are left for God to act in.

(ii) From a rather different point of view one might fully accept a scientifically explicable world with no 'gaps', yet find 'religious' experience and so the activity of God (whose precise sphere and mode of existence may be left open) as one of the whole range of human experiences of the world. This was, in effect, the Schleiermacher approach and the approach of the majority of the long line of Liberal theologians since his day, history in general and the historical Jesus in particular being part of the 'experience'. If 'religious' experience as *sui generis* offered difficulties, not least because it might not, in the light of the contemporary consciousness, seem as universal as had been supposed, and also because it might seem to be susceptible of a 'natural' explanation, then one might (with Kant) posit religious experience as being really in essence *moral* experience whose universality is at least better attested. One might, indeed, use this as the basis for a fresh attempt to define it in a religious form located in the person of Christ.

(2) The other possibility, which seems to be fore-

shadowed in Jowett, and Arnold (if Professor Braithwaite is correct[74]), is partly suggested by the position last mentioned. The nature of ethical experience may itself be questioned in the course of modern philosophical discussions of the status of moral judgements. Such judgements may be regarded as nothing more than 'attitudes' or 'stances' that are taken up towards a particular way of life or moral action; and it may be considered as nothing more than a personal choice which has no validity beyond its being just that; still less as pointing to an objective moral order; least of all as pointing towards the existence of a 'transcendent God'. If, in any case, a particular kind of moral 'stance' is adopted, then it may be visualized and indeed inculcated in various ways, and in this case 'religion' might come in as a morally useful mythology for this kind of purpose, Jesus being a case in point. This is very nearly the position in fact adopted by, for example, the 'Death of God' school. But one is then faced with the question of what 'reality' there is behind the 'stance' or 'values' adopted: the judgements made are of 'value', not of objective existence – God is certainly not 'there'; one is once more in an essentially Feuerbachian situation. Nor can one, without the risk of abusing language and one's integrity, go on to speak theologically or use traditional spiritual observances like prayer. If this general line of thought is applied by taking the scientific account of the universe seriously as complete in its own way, and then at the same time positing a view of it as 'from God', the charge may again be levelled that one is choosing an attitude which has no further status or validation.[75]

(3) It may be that a third possibility should be considered. This is the position suggested by Kierkegaard and by Existentialism since then, though it should be observed that this means it has atheist as well as Christian forms, so that the 'leap of faith' to 'authentic existence' in what amounts

to a moment of personal and even cosmic vision may or may not be a leap into a sense of God and above all Christ's God. (One supposes that some such act is also necessary in the case of Bonhoeffer's final line of thought.) No innate moral experience as a ladder to God seems allowed here, yet all the same there is a sense in which this line of thought too is an approach to living through a search for moral experience and so potentially of religious experience also. It may be concluded, then, that a search for religious experience, for all its difficulties, is the most hopeful line to God at present.

(b) The Theory and Practice of Spirituality

It has seemed convenient to treat some movements under this head rather than in the more narrowly theological context of the last section, although in the main we are now discussing points of view which do imply some version of more conservative theological positions which have to be set beside the more radical ones.

One of the most interesting and important attempts at a renewal of spirituality in the 19th century was certainly the Oxford Movement and the Anglo-Catholic tradition in the Church of England which developed from it. No doubt it begs many questions to see this as part of 'Protestantism' at all, though it grew and survived within a Church which on any reckoning was then regarded as Protestant and has continued in part to be so reckoned and therefore ought to be considered in this context. The very fact that some felt the need to make Anglicanism less Protestant in the traditional sense has a significance for our theme. Although the whole movement can be interpreted as a political and social as well as a religious reaction away from the modern world into medievalism[76] it was at least a conscious attempt to deal with the problems of the Protestant tradition and its piety, particularly as they had begun to be sharpened by changes in society.

For our purposes the basic principles of the original movement might be summed up like this: First, it was an expression of the 19th-century search for authority and objective certainty in Christianity in face of the decline we have described in certainty about the unseen, supernatural world. This may be seen in the reassertion of dogma based on Scripture as authoritatively interpreted by the early Church, as against what were felt to be the corruptions of Rome, and the subjective vagaries of Liberals and Evangelicals. It is also seen in the assertion of a visible, authoritative Church, whose means of grace are assured by an authorized hierarchy in the Apostolic Succession: this is well expressed in the famous Keble sermon on 'National Apostasy' in 1833 which was a reaction to the threat of the State treating the Church as a purely human corporation. The same concern appears in the assertion of a Real Presence of Christ in the Eucharist which, with other sacraments, links the invisible supernatural world with the visible and tangible world through physical and effective symbols: this against the long decline of the sacramental and symbolic elements of religion in Protestantism. The whole question of certainty in religious knowledge was very much involved in the movement: as against the prevailing rationalism inherited from the last century, these men felt religious knowledge depended partly on the ability to discern spiritual things by a purified mind and so it was linked with worship; whereas for some now it might rather be true to say that worship seems to depend on the possibility of belief.[77]

The other main element in the movement follows from what has just been said: a concern with the meaning and inculcation of a real, progressive and supernatural holiness in the believer especially by sacramental means, as against what was felt to be the neglect of it by Liberals and Evangelicals, who left men either self-satisfied, or relying on mere feeling, or trusting to God to save them without any real effort or any real change in their characters.[78] To achieve these ends the theological basis of the characteristically 'Catholic' scheme of salvation was adopted: salvation through a process beginning in baptism, continued through confession and the Eucharist, rather than by the act of justification experienced through an 'evangelical' conversion. And along with this went a 'Catholic' ideal of otherworldly sanctity which involved the traditional ascetic ideals and methods, pastoral discipline, and for some the eventual restoration of the specialized piety of the monastic or other religious communities. It was in many respects, therefore, a recovery within Protestantism of 'Catholic' doctrine and spirituality.

The results in worship accompanied a wider awakening to the needs of order, decency and intensity in church life: a new style of parish priest appeared (with Keble as a model), more obviously religious, theological and ascetic (though perhaps also more remote) than his predecessor of the previous century. Worship for High Churchmen was concentrated more on the Eucharist and preparation for it, for some by the confessional. The trend was carried further in the next generation, but the question will be raised whether, despite some successes, this revival extended far enough to save the faith and practice of more than a minority within the Church. It failed to revive the nation (as Methodism had also failed) and it also failed to offer a convincing picture of a piety thought out in terms of the conditions and consciousness of the emerging new world.[79]

This becomes increasingly clear in the generation after Newman's departure to Rome in 1845. That generation fought its way through controversies over eucharistic vestments and ornaments, reservation of the sacrament and eucharistic devotions, sacramental confession. They were more obviously 'Roman' in their behaviour and had to borrow a great deal from that source (particularly in its French form). They were, in fact, establishing in much more violently visual and tangible terms the sacramental principles of worship embodying the 'Catholic' religious scheme revived by the original Tractarians. In particular they were establishing a piety centred above all on the belief in the Real Presence of Christ in the Eucharist, which assures the worshipper of communion with God, salvation, the reality of God's action in the world: i.e. an answer to the problem of religious certainty and so the possibility of worship in a secular age.[80] At the same time this provided a focus for private piety lacking in the bare worship even of Anglican Protestantism.

Another aspect of the 19th-century spiritual dilemma may be seen in the Anglo-Catholic slum priests and other missioners: this was the problem of parochial care and evangelism which was linked with the problem of belief and worship. Consider, for example, the statement of one of them, Arthur Stanton: 'The basis of Ritualism', he said, 'was a belief that all human flesh was lovable and venerable, because CHRIST had worn the human form, . . .' Confession he 'championed as the only means by which a spiritual director could give individual guidance to his people: "mere preaching was like talking to a flock of sheep"'.[81] As they moved into the slums these men found the parish system of the rural past had broken down socially and religiously: one solution (tried by Anglo-Catholic and also other churchmen in various forms) was the use of 'missions' of (for Anglo-Catholics at least) a peculiarly 'Catholic' kind. Men were called to an intense repentance and forgiveness of sins centred around a recall to baptism and its renewal through sacramental penance and the Eucharist.[82]

One important advantage of this technique both in

evangelism and in pastoral practice was indicated in Stanton's remark just cited: it led to a closer pastoral supervision than mere preaching. Yet, as was said earlier, the results for the laity, and above all beyond the Church's fringe, were meagre. The Catholic imagery was an artificial creation after a long period of religion practically without symbol. It had to be *explained* – a process almost fatal to symbolism as a deep-level psychological agency. (We shall revert to this point later in discussing the Liturgical Movement.)

Another basic difficulty is not only the symbolism involved in a sacramental piety but its theological basis which becomes difficult for Protestants and not least in a non-supernaturalist era. Finally, there was the overall difficulty of an essentially 'other-worldly' piety. The late 19th-century Anglo-Catholics (or at least some of them) turned to more social and activist versions of Christianity, which, however, did not develop anything like a fresh piety for the industrial world or even anything comparable to the worker priests in 20th-century France.[83]

In turning to more specifically 'Protestant' types of spirituality, it will be recalled that its theological and practical history so far has revealed certain perennial problems inherent in the original movement which its subsequent history illustrated very forcibly. Added to this have been the characteristically modern intellectual and social pressures which were most directly faced by Liberal and other Protestants so far considered.

For more 'orthodox' and conservative Protestants the problems of the modern period have proved especially difficult. 'Evangelicals' in particular depended on a scheme of doctrine which was regarded as authorized by a literally interpreted Bible. Men were viewed as helplessly lost in Original Sin inherited from the Fall; salvation was made possible by the atonement of Christ seen as wrought by penal substitution; and it was activated in the believer through faith and experience, perhaps in a specific conversion. Thereafter one was supported by the traditional Protestant spirituality of prayer and Bible reading plus the public exercises of preaching, prayer and hymns – with a probably minimal use of the Lord's Supper interpreted in a memorialist fashion. Now it was just this scheme and its bases which was undermined most seriously by developments since the Enlightenment: that is, by biblical, moral and scientific criticism. The Liberals tried to reinterpret the Bible and the doctrines drawn from it; the Tractarians depended less exclusively on the Bible and more on the Church's tradition for the essential doctrines which they shared with the Evangelicals.

All these groups, then, were faced with a crisis of authority, but attempted to meet it in different ways. One extreme Evangelical way was that of Revivalism in its various forms from the Americans, Finney and later Moody and Sankey, to the late 19th-century Holiness movements and the Pentecostalists since 1904. All of these offered, amongst other things, what might seem to be tangible evidence that at least the traditional scheme of salvation (despite modern critics) 'worked' in actually converting people. They also seemed to offer a more exciting spiritual experience of worship, and some opportunity for personal commitment. The actual results, however, were no less, and probably in the long run, much more meagre than those of the Oxford Movement tradition – to which they were in any case inferior in their potential 'follow-up' and their ability to offer a definite scheme of progressive spirituality.[84] Nor were they any more successful in going much beyond the Protestant Evangelical church constituency with its middle-class ethos.

In fact, Protestantism seemed well on the way to losing

the effectiveness of the distinctive evangelical piety it had inherited from the past. In the days of Puritanism and of the Evangelical Revival – above all, in the Revival's Methodist form – there was at least an implied scheme of a long process of conviction and conversion from sin; and the Methodists had added to this their doctrine of a progressive and real holiness cultivated by Protestant techniques. The intensity of this way of salvation steadily dwindled or became a conventional stereotype in the 19th century.[85] Even the Methodists steadily reduced their demands from those of a chain of holiness societies to those of a mere church membership. The same was true of the large membership of all Churches which did not even choose revivalism. The Nonconformist version of a gospel with a 'social' dimension in the form of the so-called Nonconformist Conscience led to a narrow moralism rather than to a contemporary spirituality. Neither at the public nor at the private level was there sufficient content in this Protestant tradition to support a declining piety; and modern attempts to replace the infallible Bible by reliance on the Church, preaching piety by sacramental piety, and home piety by church or Sunday School piety, have manifestly failed to bite.

This sketchy survey of some of the characteristic developments in thought and piety has now carried us into the present day and, it is hoped, has helped to lay bare the roots of the contemporary crisis in religion of which the problem of a modern spirituality is a symptom as well as a part. In the final chapter we shall attempt an analysis of the situation in the categories laid down in the Introduction, with a view to making clear what the difficulties and possibilities really are, the strengths and weaknesses of some of the solutions which have been offered, and the decisions which can be and should be made.

5. Problems and Possibilities in Contemporary Spirituality

A. The Climate for Contemporary Spirituality: 'Secularization'

1. Sociological Approaches to Religion

The concept of secularization, though now fairly freely used by those in other disciplines, has primarily been developed as a sociological concept and therefore the senses in which it is used and the limits of its application by sociologists need to be made clear. It has already been pointed out (above, p. 18) that the sociological approach to religion does not pass judgement on theology, but regards religion primarily as an institutional phenomenon: that is, while it assumes that religion has its institutional side and that this side is subject to the same modes of action and analysis as any other institution, it may still be true that other dimensions of religion exist which can be considered from other angles. It must be recognized that a certain bias

97

in favour of a total secular interpretation of religion tends to be built into such analyses: that is, if a sociological explanation of religious behaviour seems to give a coherent explanation of religious behaviour, then it may be concluded that there is nothing else to explain and that therefore the supernatural is a superfluous hypothesis (the familiar dilemma). Even where this is not explicitly assumed, there are other biases which tend to be inherent in this approach.[1] Religious sociologists naturally tend to assume an identity between 'religion' and 'church'; otherwise an institutional analysis is difficult, if not impossible. This means, however, that an analysis of religious behaviour and even of belief in terms of statistics of church attendance, membership and adherence to 'beliefs' of a simple dogmatic kind tends to dominate the picture. The more highly institutionalized Churches bulk large. The social embodiment of the Church tends to be seen in terms of, for example, the traditional parish type of structure as a socio-religious community. Consequently a picture of 'secularization' of society in terms of the decline of the more obviously institutional aspect of religion and its influence on society is easy to build up; while areas where institutional religion is doing better, for example, the United States, might seem to show the opposite tendency from secularization. The possibility of religion surviving in other forms is discounted, since it is seen as tied to 'church' manifestations, particularly of a traditional kind. Belief or disbelief in traditional dogmas is a criterion which may give a bias in favour of interpreting any rejection of traditional dogma as a move to secular unbelief.

All this raises two important questions for any sociological analysis of religion: first, what it is in religion which *can* be institutionalized, and to what extent this can be institutionalized, second (and this is a purely sociological question, though one with an important bearing on our theme), the way in which any analysis of social function is conceived, for there are those who see institutions – the significance and the causes of their changes – largely in terms of the 'function' they perform. This ought not to involve any question of their more ultimate causes and significance ('supernatural' or otherwise) but can easily seem to do so. Moreover, the institutions of society, including its religious institutions, may be expected to change according to social need and social change and may affect the personal life and consciousness of men in so far as this is a product of environmental rather than genetic factors. It is for these reasons that some would raise the possibility that even subjective religion as well as religious institutions may be socially conditioned, even if not socially determined.[2]

How far, then, can a sociological analysis of religion go, and what light is this likely to throw on the present condition of religion and of spirituality in particular? The discussion so far has suggested that it may go a very long way, even if the ultimate truth of religion as supernaturally based is left an open question. Thus Helmut Schelsky has said[3] that sociology can deal only with the changing social manifestations of Christianity and not with its ultimate faith; but he distinguishes three somewhat far-reaching inquiries (and corresponding reform projects) within this limitation: first, the changing of the organizational forms and methods of the Churches (e.g. the decline of the parish and devising of other structures); then, changes in the content of Christian teaching (so as to penetrate the modern world); finally, the changing of the forms of faith (to take account of the changing forms of consciousness and inner life of modern men). In all these fields, he would claim, the changes that have taken place anyway, and changes that the Churches would like to undertake, are subject to sociological

99

analysis; and this clearly goes beyond a narrowly 'institutional' approach.

The fundamental questions raised by these investigators are: whether the types of (socially-conditioned) personality produced by modern industrial civilization allow the continuation of traditional religious patterns; what religious patterns they do allow; and how far and in what way new patterns of religion can emerge. One need not agree with the particular views of these investigators as to the content of the 'modern consciousness' to accept the general validity of their view that this consciousness has changed, that it is affected by social factors, and that this must be taken into account for spirituality. It is the failure to take these factors seriously which has helped to weaken the force of much church reform, and has led us in this essay to attempt some analysis of the changes in consciousness which have taken place and their significance. At this point we can turn to the specific thesis of 'secularization'.

2. The Concept of Secularization

The terms in which this is described vary but the phenomenon in mind is recognizably the same. Harvey Cox[4] sees it as implying a historical process, almost certainly irreversible, in which society and culture are delivered from tutelage to religious control and closed metaphysical world-views (compare Bonhoeffer's 'man's coming of age' and 'autonomy'). A Roman Catholic, Thomas O'Dea,[5] speaks of two related transformations in human thinking: the 'desacralization' of our attitudes to persons and things, and the 'rationalization of thought' by which there is a 'withholding of emotional participation' in thinking about the world. As a result, the religious world-view is no longer the basic frame of reference for thought; a view of the world as no longer sacred, and as composed of things to be manipulated, arises, which at best crowds the religious view into the 'private' area of experience. Bryan Wilson[6] speaks of 'the process whereby religious thinking, practice and institutions lose social significance'; and his description of how this involves religious practice as well as institutions and their influence in the world shows how far the effects extend – as Luckmann and Schelsky also claim. Wilson points out that 'even if, as some sociologists have argued, non-logical behaviour continues' perpetually to operate in society and some might see this as a continuing basis for religion, 'then at least the terms of non-rationality have changed'. It is no longer Christian dogmas which dictate behaviour, but other 'irrational and arbitrary assumptions'.[7]

It should be added that although much religious practice remains – and for religious reasons – this is held to be a declining force and the processes which have led to its decline will operate increasingly and over wider areas as industrialization (in particular) advances. What these processes are we have already described more than once (see especially Chapter 4). Whatever explanation is given of these phenomena, and whether or not the process is irreversible, it is hard to deny that the phenomena exist. Whether 'secularization' is an appropriate word for them, whether they are all part of the same unitary process, whether they have caused the equally evident contemporary decline in religious institutions, and how far this affects the substance of religion itself – these are more debatable questions.[8]

The most serious challenge so far to the whole thesis of secularization is presented by David Martin.[9] He argues that the thesis uses and confuses two approaches.

(a) The use of a definition of religion according to 'conventional usage' – in terms of institutions like Churches, which are taken to be in decline. 'Decline' would be a better word than 'secularization' but in any case to show it has happened one would have to show it in relation to institutions having some common characteristics, a demonstration which, he believes, is very difficult to carry out. He concludes that no unitary process called 'secularization' arises in reaction to a set of characteristics called 'religious'; for religious institutions bear no such common characteristics.

(*b*) The second approach is by way of an analytic criterion for differentiating the real or genuine elements in religion from the bogus. A wide range of criteria could be used; other-worldly *versus* this-worldly; metaphysical *versus* positive; mythopoeic *versus* factual; miraculous *versus* law-abiding; conditional *versus* ineluctable. This raises the problem of whether a single criterion can be used as a basis for analysis, or whether groups of criteria can be linked together. Both possibilities run up against historical difficulties; and any pair are open to the objection that they are not exclusively identifiable with 'religious' and 'secular' views respectively. Hence the criteria for differentiating two outlooks break down. In any case the rise and decline of institutions occurs for a variety of reasons, and the decline of religious institutions may simply reflect the difficulties of *all* social institutions in an age of rapid change.[10]

Martin concludes that as there is no unitary process of secularization, so one cannot talk in a unitary way about the causes of secularization. He considers that the whole concept is a tool of 'counter-religious ideologies' which identify the 'real' element in religion for polemical purposes and arbitrarily relate it to a unitary and irreversible process of decline. As prime examples of such 'ideologies' he cites Marxism, and what he calls 'Rationalism' and 'Existentialism'. He then proceeds to explode their pretensions and concludes there is a good future for religion because of the continuing element of non-rationality in human nature.

These arguments have cogency, and some of the charges

are at least partially true of some of those using the concepts concerned. Martin, however, uses very rigid categories of judgement on what he calls the 'unitary processes' of 'religion' and 'secularization'; the point here is that the material dealt with is a mixture of sociology and history, and in both fields what has to be done is to set up verifiable hypotheses about examinable sets of facts. Whether the material ever allows of the kind of results achievable in the natural sciences is certainly open to question. But that some such procedure is indispensable if one is to attempt any explanation of events at all seems self-evident; Martin himself does it – and his categories of 'Rationalism' and 'Existentialism' are as open (some would say more open) to his own objections to the concept of 'secularization', conceptually speaking.

The thesis is such that it is appropriately tested partly on historical grounds, and much information is still lacking even for the more superficial indexes like church attendance. Still, enough is available to show the trend at any rate for the last century or so – which is downward; and even the American example does not count against this unless one actually *assumes* that membership *per se* is a final index of the religious condition (if Martin really stuck to this he ought to concede that religion *has* steadily weakened in Western Europe). Martin has to concede that when one takes into account the evidence of the last 200–300 years one does detect a drastic change towards the ideas held of God, the world, and the supernatural, and many would argue that this (which Martin does concede) is not to be reduced in significance to a fad of a few intellectuals (see above, p. 16) The 'secular' outlook delineated by the upholders of the thesis cannot be dismissed as an illusion: however difficult to express as a 'unitary' process, the basic fact of a world viewed (even in its 'irrational' moods) as a

103

set of phenomena to be given a non-religious, non-transcendental, non-sacred explanation is the basic outlook of the contemporary West and not solely for intellectuals.[11] The difficulties this has created for religion are real, as we attempted to show in the last chapter, even at the level of institutions. The *prima facie* case for associating these difficulties with industrialization (even for the U.S.A.) has been suggested by Luckmann[12]: he notes differences in church allegiance between town and country, between women and men, between middle-aged (working) population and the very old and very young, class and work differences. As to the charge that the thesis is 'ideological', one can agree with Wilson[13] that theologians and others who would not *prima facie* wish to prove that religion is in such difficulties have accepted the thesis as being a correct analysis even though they recognize that it might be put forward also for reasons, and in a form, affected by ideological considerations. To dismiss such theologians as simply suffering from masochism does not prove anything – any more than the charge which might be levelled at critics of the thesis that they do not wish to admit that religion may be in decline. Whatever is thought of the thesis as a whole, and whatever criticisms one may make about the prejudices of those who hold it, one needs to recognize the reality of the phenomena which have provoked it and take them into account for spirituality.

3. Social Change, Secularization and Spirituality

Social change – whether or not one speaks of its overall relation to religion as one of 'secularization' – has, we have suggested, operated in two ways or at two levels.[14] At the *institutional* level the Church has become marginal to society: if it makes its traditional religious and moral claims on men it seems to act as if its old place in society still existed;

if it tries to adapt to new social and psychological functions it is in danger of having to dissolve its old institutions. At the level of *subjective religion* one has to consider the possibility of changes in personal consciousness no longer readily corresponding to existing church life. The question arises whether the contemporary consciousness is 'institutionalizable' at all, least of all in a religious institution.

Church institutions have become simply one among many types of institution, representing one of many world-views, none of which is comprehensive, and all of which are rationalized according to function. In so far as religion is still a possible personal and private way of looking at the world, it not only lacks an absolute and universal value but also is badly structured to carry out any such claim since it is often tied to the forms of a traditional social order. There is, too, a serious lack of correspondence between the reality of the present consciousness (including the religious consciousness) of men and the consciousness implied in normal institutionalized religious practice: it is a commonplace of investigations into the outlook of church-attached people to find them conforming to the goals and consciousness of the rest of society of their type.

While the world generally lacks a comprehensive value-system and a world of common symbolism linked with it, this is also becoming true of Christians – which hits the Church and Christianity hard, for transcendent religious symbolism has also broken down. Nothing as clear and comprehensive as the old myth of the Fall has emerged to fit contemporary experience; and the same is true of symbols of worship and spirituality. Under the old Christian (verbal and visual) vocabulary exist, very often, more 'worldly' notions; and attempts at revaluation, as we have seen, raise the question of whether the same thing (above all, whether something 'supernatural') is being talked about at all.

This is one reason for the decline of church-centred religion which may well be a significant factor in contemporary religion. Kierkegaard and Bonhoeffer hinted at this in different ways; the 'Death of God' theologian, Hamilton, shows little interest in the 'church' question at all. It may be that one important strain in a future spirituality will be a dissociation of individual and personal religion from normal 'church' institutions altogether; that is, if this is possible (the question is further discussed below, p. 134ff).[15]

But the fundamental difficulty remains: can one conceive of God, as a 'supernatural' being implying some kind of 'supernatural' order with which spirituality connects us, in anything like the traditional way, if the traditional ways of viewing and believing these things seem ruled out by modern ways of viewing the world? This, we have seen, has been the underlying preoccupation of the more alert thinkers of the last two hundred years or so; and this has been a major element in the talk about secularization. The problem in relation to spirituality has been usefully raised by Claude Geffré in an article mentioned earlier in the discussion of recent Roman Catholic theology.[16] He speaks of 'desacralization', which is a description of one major element in a secularized view of the world; and he considers that any spirituality arising out of this world will be one in which the world is 'accepted', will be of a 'post-religious world of faith', and will be of 'an anonymous charity'. Geffré concentrates his interest on the first of these and discusses in particular the relation between the 'sacred' and the 'profane'. How far, he asks, does the process of desacralization serve holiness? should it be opposed, in favour of re-creating 'sacred regions' in which faith can take root?[17] His problem is essentially the one we have seen as haunting the post-Kantian world and notably recognized by Bonhoeffer: to find a 'space' for God and so for spirituality.

Geffré discusses two opposed viewpoints on the matter in Roman Catholic discussions, which will serve very well to illustrate basic alternatives. He cites Fr Chenu as seeing the progress of Christianity towards a Church which is purely a 'presence in the world'. The aim is to 'Christianize the world as it grows': not to build a 'Christian world' alongside the secular one, but rather to promote the natural growth of the secularized world and to work through its freedom. The modern trend is against 'religion' and one criticizes 'religion' as part of the interpretation of 'faith' (compare Barth and Bonhoeffer).

The other point of view is represented by Jean Daniélou, who has stated that there can be no Christianity without 'Christendom'. There is a need to defend the substance of the 'sacred' wherever it is found, even in superstitious and 'bad' religion (partly for the sake of 'simple' Christians). The world must be resacralized before it can be sanctified.[18]

As Geffré says, the basic issue between the two views is whether the world must be 'resacralized' before it can be sanctified (if, we might add, this is possible); or whether the present process of desacralization can create an opportunity for the authentic revival of Christianity (if, we might add, there is any alternative). (The points we have added are a reminder that if areas of 'mystery' occur in the modern world they are unlikely to be seen as 'sacred' or as evidence of the 'supernatural' in any case.) Geffré himself inclines to Chenu's view with an important proviso. He accepts desacralization as a fact; he accepts a critique of 'religion'. But he believes that a basic 'sacredness' does exist even as a basis for the 'profane' world, in the mystery of 'creation' itself. There is an 'original sacredness of creation, which is precisely the mystery of man, a sort of openness towards the transcendent'. The sacred is not a 'thing' but a relationship, co-extensive with all being and reality. 'If the Word of God is to find a point of contact with man in our desacralized civilization we cannot restore an archaic and illusory sacredness, but we *must* restore that *original sacredness* (of creation), that sacredness which coincides with the truth of man as a mystery of openness to transcendence.' He accepts the de-mystification of the old ultimates of birth and death in an explicable and controllable universe: there is no longer any 'space' for God as 'useful' to men. What is left? The very fact of de-mystification provokes the question 'What for?', the sense of the absurd in the human condition. Hence we may 'create in ourselves a "space for being queried" '; and we need to restore to its full value the domain of human existence and the possibilities opened up by encounter with other people. 'Sacredness' may be found as the basis of faith in the sense of 'the original truth of man as a mystery of receptiveness and commission' – and so we may become receptive to the Other through the other.

There is much in this approach which is reflected also in Brian Wicker's use of M. Eliade's views on the 'sacred' and the 'profane',[19] though Wicker emphasizes the community sense as fundamental for the individual. Of this whole approach two things at least need to be said. There is more than a hint of the assumption that there exists in man an innate 'religious sense' which will perpetually renew itself. (Geffré's 'original sacredness' in creation, his 'openness towards the transcendent' seems uncommonly like this, unless it is to be taken simply as a 'capacity' in the sense we defined in Chapter 2.) But if (as both Geffré and Wicker imply) what we build on is simply the ordinary built-in sense of the 'other' which we feel in individual personal encounters or as part of a community, this (if it exists) has no necessary religious or 'faith' connotation or connexion at all. Like all else in the world, it is perfectly capable of being seen, and need only be seen, as a human, secular phenomenon with no further implications. Geffré, unlike Wicker (although the latter draws heavily on Marx for his own purposes) fully recognizes the criticism of religion from Feuerbach through Marx, Nietzsche and Freud as radical attacks on 'the illusions of consciousness'. These have, he acknowledges, 'become some of the ways along which any meditation on the faith must pass'.

Despite the criticisms we have just made of Geffré's approach it must be acknowledged that he has seen the issues for a modern spirituality in all their seriousness. He sums up: there is room for criticism of 'religion' as an attempt at self-justification or a refusal to accept responsibility for one's own life. But (and this is the point) the denial of faith as rooted in a religious dimension of man and necessarily expressing itself in a religious manner, leads to deadlock. He adds (and our analysis of theologians' treatment of the point bears him out) that prayer is a 'decisive criterion to unmask the ambiguities of "non-religious" Christianity'. (In his use of 'religion' Geffré does not altogether avoid this ambiguity.)

It is in the light of this dilemma (which underlies the other problems so far outlined in this chapter as the characteristic problems of a 'secularized' age) that we shall now proceed to discuss the possibilities of a modern spirituality. In doing so, it should by now be clear, we are accepting the view that the phenomena described collectively as 'secularization' do exist, are likely to persist, and pose the problems for religion which we have indicated. But in accepting this it should be emphasized that the process is not necessarily to be seen as totally evil and to be resisted at all costs – even if this were possible. On the contrary it may be seen as, on the whole, good and to be welcomed if it liberates men from concentration on dead forms of religious thought and practice which have tended to obscure God and evade confrontation with him – as Kierkegaard and Bonhoeffer amongst others suggested. The real enemies (it has been suggested[20]) are 'secularism' as an ideological world-view and 'materialism' which is closely akin to it: in both cases moral, let alone religious criticism of the existing aims of society is ruled out.

B. The Forms of a Contemporary Spirituality

As a framework for the rest of this chapter the mode of analysis proposed in the first chapter is adopted, within which the various problems and possibilities are discussed. It will be recalled that the analysis was in the following terms:

(1) The Aim: i.e., what is the proper 'model' of the Christian life?

(2) The Types: i.e., what kinds of piety (for example, corporate or individual, sacramental or non-sacramental) are to be followed?

(3) The Conditions: i.e., under what conditions may or should a particular model and type of piety be worked out, especially 'in' or 'out of' the world?

(4) The Means or Methods: i.e. in the main, what particular techniques are to be used?

In discussing these categories earlier it was pointed out that the crucial distinction was to be drawn between the 'aim' or 'model' on the one hand, and the means adopted to achieve it on the other, the former to be considered as primary. The category of 'conditions' was to be seen as a middle term between the two; and in all these cases the 'model' adopted was considered liable to settle some at least of the 'conditions' and 'means' which are possible; but so, it should by now be realized, does the climate of our time as it has been described earlier in this essay.

1. The Aim or Model of Spirituality

This, we have suggested, is the really primary thing to be settled, but it is often taken for granted that there is no problem here and that one can go on immediately to discuss techniques, at which point disagreements arise. In fact there is often serious, though concealed, disagreement on the aim or model of Christianity.

It may be suggested that two questions are involved here: (*a*) where is the Christian model to be found, and on what grounds? and (*b*) what is the content of this model?

As regards (*a*), this involves all the problems we have constantly had in mind about 'revelation', 'the transcendent', a 'space' for God and so on for anyone who asserts a supernatural standard; though for that matter anyone who asserts one ideal as superior to another faces equally difficult questions of justification. One extra problem faces the Christian, that of justifying the choice of Jesus as the paradigm for God, the authority for religious and moral behaviour. As in morality, so in religion, the question is, Why this particular choice? – and as Kierkegaard showed, there can be no historical demonstration making such a choice inevitable, even though it may be shown to be reasonable. In the last resort it is an act of faith; just as for some modern moral philosophers, the choice of a morality is a personal choice of a stance which cannot ultimately be shown to be more valid than any other. To choose Jesus as the model for life is one possible form of moral choice, and this is at least no less valid a possibility than any other.

A Christian will normally, however, wish to say more: he will wish to claim that the choice of Jesus is, in fact, a religious and not merely a moral choice. That is to say, a belief in God is implied, and in Jesus as the sign of a particular kind of belief in a particular view of God; and, further, that such a choice is to lead to religious as well as to moral activity. Two difficulties arise here: one is the general difficulty of establishing belief in God; and the other is to establish a difference between morality and religion, especially if religion is taken to require a belief in God as transcendent. But if this belief is not held, religion seems simply to be a form of morality – no more and no less. Here we may recall Arnold's solution and Braithwaite's version of it (above, p. 77): religion is 'morality touched by emotion' or 'reinforced' by the adoption of certain 'myths' or 'parables'. A Christian is distinguished by the particular 'myths' he adopts and by the source from which he draws them, the personal model they propose – that is, Jesus. The 'Death of God' types of theology really do this: the concept of 'God' is regarded as no longer tenable; the transcendent has vanished in its traditional sense. What is left is the use of the term 'Christianity' ostensibly at least as a religious rather than a merely moral usage, which usage is justified by the adoption of 'Jesus' rather than some other person or ideal as normative. Jesus, however, is seen (see next section) as 'the man for others' rather than as 'God' or 'divine'. It is evident that in this usage 'Jesus' is in fact being used to fulfil the functions of 'God' or of 'the transcendent' in that he is taken as the absolute standard of a particular way of life (call it morality or religion as you will). Either this implies simply a 'stance' adopted without the possibility of rational demonstration; or it is a concealed claim to revelation. But it may well be that it is only in such ways that one can for the moment approach one's choice of a 'model'.

(b) If Jesus is, in some sense, taken to be the model of the Christian life, then we must ask what the content of this model is: what pattern of belief and life is implied. To be a Christian does seem to involve, as a starting-point, the acceptance at least of Jesus, rather than any other, as the model. Can one then reject belief in God, however difficult this belief may at the moment be to conceive? For Jesus certainly took this as central – he points to himself not as an end but as a means, at most as a paradigm, for God's will. But in any case what kind of life – the life of God – is Jesus concerned to show? Here arguments about concepts of 'vision of God', 'communion with God', 'salvation', and 'discipleship', no doubt have their place, but it may be suggested that the fundamental choice is between the model of the First Great Commandment and of the Second Great Commandment as normative. It should at once be added that by putting the issue in this way one does not imply that the two are mutually exclusive. On the contrary both are clearly binding in Jesus' teaching; and the question is rather of which comes first and which is most likely to lead to the other or to include the other. Our basic contention will be that traditional piety (perhaps most clearly, in the long run, in Catholicism) put the First Commandment as primary, and as the commandment from which consequences on the lines of the Second would flow. But much modern (and notably Protestant) piety has begun from the Second and evaded the First for reasons which have already been hinted at and will be made plain in a moment.

(i) *Concentration on the First Commandment* might be described in several ways. For example, Kierkegaard saw it as the 'absolute relation to the Absolute', and here he was in principle restating the classical Catholic ideal which 'makes the relationship with God the all-important one, and insists that it must be perfected'.[21] In much Catholic piety this seemed to involve an absolute 'renunciation' of the world in monasticism or one of its adaptations. We shall see later (under 'Types') that this raises as many problems as it solves, yet the ideal of 'forsaking' the world to concentrate on God may be right, even though it may not involve the physical departure from the world to the cloister which has normally been assumed as necessary.

But the main point is to decide whether the First Great Commandment is the primary aim. Now it is evident that it is no longer the primary consideration in much modern spirituality – even in Roman Catholicism. The reasons for this are historically of two kinds. First, there is the development of Protestantism which originally was a protest in favour of this absolute devotion to God, but which coupled this with a rejection of the spirituality of renunciation and monasticism which had most clearly embodied the ideal, in favour of a piety in the world. But we have seen that Protestants failed to develop an effective alternative to Catholic piety and, instead, allowed the development of a progressive identification of the will of God with total immersion in the world, and so ultimately with merely 'worldly' standards. But there is a second reason for this which has operated quite apart from any weaknesses in Protestantism, though it has affected that type of Christianity most quickly. In the circumstances of secularization we have already described, the very terms of the First Commandment ideal become suspect: God, above all as a transcendent, supernatural being, seems increasingly difficult to believe in. And so suspicion falls on all the traditional methods (Protestant as well) because their essential alignment to a relationship with God and not merely with man, or with an ideal in a man's mind, has become obscured.

So the development of society and the decline in the felt reality of God lead to an emphasis on our relationship, implicit or explicit, with men, and one has then the substitution of the Second Great Commandment of loving one's brother. This may or may not include the assumption that you thereby love the invisible God as a kind of by-product.

(ii) *Concentration on the Second Commandment* is the result of living in a 'secularized' world; and the general effect of such a concentration is to turn Christianity into ethics, Christian piety being then either identified with this or seen as a by-product of it. In either case what often needs to be questioned is the brand of ethics which, divested of its 'supernatural' or 'absolute' reference, is proffered as 'Christian'. This weakness is not always obvious: for a decline in certainty about God as the object of piety may actually be masked by, for example, a concern for, and devotion to the Church which, as we have seen, has in this century become a feature even of Churches which have traditionally emphasized individual experience of God. The attack of a Kierkegaard on 'Christendom' or of a Bonhoeffer on 'religion' is at least partly explicable as a realization of the dangers of this: it may be an evasion of the difficulties (and demands) of God; and Churches may too easily approximate in their aims to merely humane concerns. And indeed this has come to be the case: religion has been re-defined not merely in terms of ethics but of social or personal ethics which are an uncritical acceptance of the aims (maybe worthy, but not necessarily even that) of contemporary society. No distinctively Christian standard is likely to appear automatically out of these preoccupations; spirituality, personal and corporate, is likely to be uncritical, lacking a standard and a method by which to examine and heighten the aims of the Christian.

In sum, then, we have lost the older models for spirituality, yet we have not found a satisfactory one to replace them. In so far as a fresh model has been found, it has been a development of human relationships rather than of a

Godward relationship[22]: i.e. the Second Great Commandment has been taken up in preference to the First. Whatever the difficulties of the old model, the new suffers from at least three serious defects: First, a model for relationships is necessary, even for human ones, and this is not always consciously recognized. Second, in so far as a model has been adopted, it is often too relaxed, and lacks the absolute aspirations of the older piety towards God and holiness. Third, the older model had the element of renunciation, rejecting some of the standards of the ordinary world. This is still necessary for the would-be Christian, as the example of Christ shows clearly enough, even if monasticism will not do as a way of expressing and achieving it.

What seems to be needed is a recovery of the First Great Commandment, involving an element of 'renunciation' of the world, yet practised in the world, as Protestantism saw. Some pointers to this may be seen in Kierkegaard and in Bonhoeffer; also, in a measure, in the worker-priest experiment. It may be asked whether it is right to be as obsessed with the fate of one's own soul as this implies. The answer is partly that one should certainly reject the obsession with ultimate salvation and damnation, which should be left as a mystery in the hands of God – where alone it can belong, for others as well as for oneself. The other point to make in answer to this problem is that one must be consciously concerned with one's own holiness in relation to Jesus, not only because otherwise one's life is left uncriticized, content with unsatisfactory standards; but also because even one's relationships with others – and so the implementation of the Second Great Commandment – depend on this. This is because of the effects of our actions on others about which we need to be made more aware, and for which we should constantly feel responsible.[23] It may be added that the continuing difficulty of belief in God, as entailed in following

116

the First Commandment as model, is partly met by the knowledge of moral change in relationship to the model followed.

Undeniably, this approach continues to raise large problems, some of which will be considered in the rest of this chapter. Apart from those just mentioned, there is the whole complex of questions centring round the size and form of Christian community which is possible if such a high ideal is upheld. Does it imply a Christian *élite*? The end of the comprehensive institutional Church? There are signs that these trends are operating anyway, for whatever reason; and that Christianity may become a minority religion in a rather drastic sense.

2. *The Types of Spirituality*

The choice of a model for piety does not automatically settle the types, conditions and means by which it is to be achieved, although it may go some way towards determining some of them. When, for convenience, 'types' of piety are distinguished, it may be felt that such a category shades into that of means, which no doubt it does. But a rough distinction is made here because there are some traditional contrasts in types of piety which are of a sufficiently fundamental character to make them more than contrasts in technique. In what follows it is recognized that the contrasts made may not in practice be mutually exclusive at all times for all individuals.

(i) *Corporate and Individual Piety:* This is a choice which may well seem still to be freely made once a basic model of Christianity has been chosen; yet it may be asked whether such a remark does not imply more right or even possibility of choice than in fact exists. One may ask, for example, how far the temperament of an individual or of a particular period of history allows such choices; and whether some forms of Christianity leave it open: for Christians often assume rather than demonstrate that Christianity necessarily involves one type or the other.

For example, it is often assumed that true worship is by nature corporate, and moreover in a more or less developed liturgical form; ideally, even private devotion finds its source in the public liturgy. One should not, it has been argued, regard the liturgy merely as 'the *official* form for the *external* worship of the Church'.[24] Much less should one regard that 'form' as carried on in separation from the private devotions of the individual worshipper which may properly be conducted while the liturgy is 'done for him'. Both Catholic and Protestant, it is urged, have been guilty of undue individualism in the past, but in the Liturgical Movement and in other ways it is said that this is being rightly overcome: corporate and individual worship should not be in antagonism, and indeed the corporate should, if anything, take priority both on biblical grounds and on the grounds of the needs of modern humanity. Thus theological and liturgical propriety seems reinforced by sociology.[25]

This point of view seems to depend on two associated assumptions: that men, through even the most drastic social psychological changes, remain basically drawn to a close communal feeling; and that they have an equally ineradicable instinct to worship in a close communal way. Both of these assumptions are open to serious question in the light of the history we have surveyed. Some sociologists have strongly argued that industrialized urban society has broken the close-knit, slowly-moving localized society of the past, which had a cohesive communal character, into a much looser network of 'associational' patterns to several of which individuals may belong. The Church, based traditionally on the older static patterns, suffers in consequence. At the same time, 'despite much that has been said to the contrary, man has no "instinct to worship", if this means that he is compulsively driven into taking part in a collective ritual directed towards a supernatural being. It should be quite clear that men and women can and do live perfectly satisfactory lives without taking part in any activities or this kind . . . for most people worship is a learned activity. . . . Since worship is learned, objective ritual would seem to be its natural form . . .'.[26]

Here we must consider the difficulties raised by modern society. A major element in corporate, as in private, worship was in the past 'ritual' in the sense of objective acts to safeguard the stability of society and in particular as a 'religious' expression of perennial physical and mental needs – e.g., crops, victory in battle, the cure of illness, the aversion of all kinds of disaster. A great deal of popular and large-scale corporate piety as well as private prayer has always operated at this level (which is not to deny that it has been mixed with more 'other-worldly' motives). But the world which has developed since the 18th century has steadily eroded the significance of, and confidence in, this motive for religious activity: a science-based world sees and solves its problems in non-supernatural, non-religious terms.

Mixed up with observances for these 'secular' purposes, taking often the same forms, and more rarely in a 'pure' form, have been the activities of men in worship directed solely to communion with God: and, not least at the popular level, these too have declined because of the difficulties already discussed about belief in God, and because of the pull towards secular ends, secularly understood. To recover corporate religious activity in either of the two senses described presents serious difficulties, but the Liturgical Movement may be seen as one such attempt.

It would be quite superficial to dismiss this either as mere antiquarianism (though there are aspects of it which involve

119

this) or, where Rome is concerned, as a belated recovery of the values of the Reformation (vernacular liturgy, communion of the people). Rather it has become the focus of a reformed theology both of worship and of society; and the detailed changes in language, ritual and architecture are to be understood as expressing this. The Mass comes to be seen as a *collective* act of worship in which priest and people are joined with one another and with Christ. It is an act in which the *redemptive* work of Christ is focused: men come from the world to sanctify their life and that of the world at the common altar in the 'worldly' and 'material' elements of bread and wine, and they go out to sanctify the world outside. In France, in particular, the Movement has also been a convenient focus for a variety of biblical, theological, evangelistic and social concerns. It is because of the underlying significance to which the Movement points that the Anglican Church has been able to borrow a good deal from it, whereas the more superficial points of vernacular and biblical interest could have been ignored as already achieved at the Reformation.[27]

Now, underlying this Movement are several assumptions which ought not to be too readily accepted. Men, it is assumed, really have a religious sense, and a corporate religious sense at that; really they *want* to worship and it is only the outdated forms of our worship and teaching that put them off: reform these and worship recovers. In particular, the Eucharist and its religious and social symbolism is, or can be made, the unquestioned centre of meaningful corporate worship, the natural expression of our religious beliefs and of our natural desire for 'community'. But are these assumptions valid? It is certainly far from clear that worship thus conceived has much impact on those alienated from Christianity or, further, that it is adequate even for a considerable section of practising Christians.

The more fundamental reasons for this include, first, the mistaken belief that urbanized modern men have, or even want to have, a 'community' sense of the old kind, and this has repercussions on church life beyond worship. The reality, it has been suggested, steadily moves towards more loosely 'associational' patterns: this need not be deplored[28] but in any case it may have to be accepted. The proclaiming of the Church and its worship as of a 'family' and 'community' nature is then badly misconceived. Second, there is a misconception about symbolism and the symbolism of the Eucharist as the centre of worship in particular. Quite apart from the fact that it may be taken to symbolize psychologically and socially mistaken aims, there is the question of whether it *can* effectively symbolize these aims. The most obvious symbolism of the Eucharist (not to mention the actual content of much, even, of the revised versions of the liturgy) points to concepts of sacrifice, sin and forgiveness, perhaps also of service – but not primarily social service, the community sense and so on. If it is felt that these concepts no longer retain their old compulsion on a generation lacking a sense of sin, then they may be reinterpreted, as indeed they are by the Liturgical Movement. But – and this is a basic difficulty – can explained and interpreted 'symbols' expressing, it is claimed, such far-reaching new ideas (which, in any event, may not be the ideas required) act in any way effectively as *symbols*? Symbols need to be simple, direct, acting almost unconsciously. Once they have to be elaborately explained, one is entering another world of communication altogether. And this raises the somewhat terrifying question of how far our secularized world any longer reacts at all readily and deeply to this kind of symbolic communication.

There is one further major objection to the use of the reinterpreted Eucharist as central to all worship, and this may serve as a bridge to the 'individual' side of the contrast which is the subject of the present discussion. For many Christians the Eucharist is by no means the centre of worship, and in so far as they use it they do so with a different significance from that of those who make it the staple diet of piety. Often associated with this 'low' Protestant view is a distaste for corporate worship in a fixed 'liturgical' form. So once again much in the Liturgical Movement fails of its effect. This general point of view has ancient roots – it is not merely Protestant nor merely a condition of modern men; and it does no good to ignore it or dismiss it as bad because it is 'individualist' and 'subjective'.[29] This tradition has been a recurring phenomenon from the days of the early Church and of medieval Catholicism and in some of its most intense forms was a strong feature of certain ascetics and mystics. The same is true of the more intense Protestant sects – and it must be recalled that even the more central Protestant tradition so distrusted the Mass that for much of Protestant history it was difficult to retain it even in the shape of frequent communion, let alone as the central focus of worship. The Protestant tradition concentrated on the Word and rather on the individual experience of its effects than on its corporate effects. Moreover, if the personal experience of the believer in his contact with God is what really counts in the end in this tradition (as for many Protestants it has done) corporateness, *however* expressed, is at best artificial and at worst inessential.

One must conclude, then, that before a revival of worship is possible, there must be a much more searching appraisal of what the psycho-social condition of men now is; at least if worshipping practice is to be effective rather than merely 'correct' – by some traditional or other arbitrary standard. It is reasonable to ask for this because it may be urged that what matters in the end is communion with

God and an effective Christian life with men – to the glory of God, and not the achievement of some alleged liturgical norm. If large-scale corporate worship is a declining possibility for this age (for reasons of a religious as well as of a social nature) then this need not be regarded as disastrous.[30]

(ii) *'Catholic' and 'Protestant'*: these tiresome terms cannot be avoided entirely, and it may be claimed that they do point to identifiable tendencies even where these are not always mutually exclusive. Some justification for making use of this contrast emerged, it is hoped, in the course of Chapter 3. Part of the content of the contrast could be described in the terms of 'corporate and individual' in the preceding paragraphs. Other contrasts (the list is far from exhaustive) include the sacramental and non-sacramental types of worship; and the priestly and prophetic types of ministry.

The *sacramental* issue is an important one, and some aspects of it have already been touched on in discussing corporate worship. One problem is the divorce of the 'material' and 'spiritual' realms as the result of the development of scientific understanding; this makes it more difficult to hold the fundamental assumption of 'Catholic' sacramentalism, i.e., that the material somehow 'conveys' the spiritual (no matter in how subtle, even metaphorical, a sense this is conceived; and the more metaphorical, the more unrealistic in some ways). Hence all attempts at a basically sacramental religion[31] are liable to fall down, particularly in the long run at the popular level. We have already noted the long-standing Protestant difficulties at this point: and these (when reinforced by characteristically modern difficulties) make any forcing of a basically sacramental form of worship on instinctively non-sacramental worshippers a delusory process. The fact is that such worship requires a far more elaborate theological justification –

123

and one which is increasingly difficult to accept if it is basically in the terms of 'conveying a presence' or of specific virtues by reason of sincere partaking – than is possible for many Protestants to endorse without self-deception.

The alternative in Protestant tradition has been to regard the fundamental sacrament as that of the 'Word'.[32] It may be that this is still a workable alternative to sacramentalism, based on a different fundamental theory of the relation of the material and the spiritual which may be seen as in better accord with the known nature of reality. This will be discussed further in connexion with prayer (below, pp. 146ff.). For the moment it should be said that it is not implied that sacramentalism is not in some sense possible for the majority, but rather that in the strong sense of material channels for the spiritual it may be difficult; and that non-sacramental worship ought not to be regarded as inferior and defective worship, nor sacramental worship as the only possible norm for Christianity: in most discussions of worship it is indeed seen in just this way.

In considering *priestly and prophetic* styles of ministry and their implications for piety, two sets of factors should be considered. The development of society is certainly away from the status and power of the Church as an institution, and this is bound to affect the status of its leaders. In a professionalized society 'the role of the clergy becomes more distinctive within religious institutions, and becomes more specifically, and more circumscribedly, religious. They become increasingly influential concerning the future of the Churches.'[33] One can see this happening as one element in the shift in non-Catholic circles towards an enhanced status for the clergy, at least in their own theological eyes. At the same time there is in some Churches a strong 'lay' as against 'ministerial' tradition for the ministries of the Church, just as there has been an anti-liturgical tradition in worship. At the present time, as is well known, there is talk in most Churches, including the Roman, about greater lay participation in the Church; though if this is no more than a matter of church activities this may only mean an enlargement of the priesthood and professional status to cover the 'ecclesiastical' laity – to make them, indeed, safely ecclesiastical and serving the organization. But any movement to reduce the scope of church-centred religion is bound to affect the status and the function of the clergy, so that the old contrast between the ministry and laity may break down.

(iii) *Other Contrasts:* these include the contrast between religion *'in'* or *'out'* *of the world* – and in this connexion one would have to consider monasticism and quasi-monastic 'rules of life'. With this question is closely associated that of different *styles of piety* – ascetic or non-ascetic, under spiritual directors or not (which has implications for the question of ministry too). The relation between *intellectual and practical* styles of life and methods of devotion would be another possible distinction of 'type'. Some remarks on these points will be made in the rest of this chapter. In each case one has to be continually aware of the two sets of influences already frequently referred to. Those arising from the non-theological, non-religious pressures of society, and those arising from pressures within the Christian community itself – which may, indeed, be based at least in part on social and psychological factors of a general kind.

3. The Conditions of Spirituality

In discussing the two basic 'models' of piety it was suggested that these could be seen in terms of the First and Second Great Commandments as representing concentration of piety on God and men respectively as the primary aim. It was suggested, next, that the difficulties now existing

125

in the first 'model' had led to a concentration on the second. The first model involved, traditionally, an element of 'renunciation' of the world, which in Catholicism has normally been taken to imply actual withdrawal from the world into a religious order or at least some approximation to this and its rules for the serious Christian even if he remained partly in the world's life. Where this whole model has been abandoned for the second model it has commonly led to forms of Christianity indistinguishable from ordinary ethics; and where some sense of a different standard has been retained it has been difficult to see how this can be maintained without returning to the conditions as well as the ideals of the first model. The question, then, is whether a return to the values of the first model, with its ideal of renunciation of the world, is possible without recalling also the conditions under which it has traditionally been pursued. We have suggested that Kierkegaard and Bonhoeffer at least seem to visualize such a renunciatory piety, centred on God yet in the world, although it must be admitted that Kierkegaard's last phase included elements recalling much in traditional asceticism (e.g. celibacy).

It must be said at once that there are still plenty of religious communities within both the Roman and the Anglo-Catholic tradition which pursue the traditional piety of the First Commandment by the traditional means: that is, either by total disconnexion from the world or by some modification within it. It must also be recognized that by their own confession they now have difficulties in finding new members and in satisfying those they have.[34] The continuation of that tradition in Catholic piety which allows of Orders which spend part of their time in the world but still under rule may be illustrated by the example of the 'Little Brothers of Jesus' inspired by Charles de Foucauld.[35] They are content with a 'presence' in the world of the workers, and a 'realization of a contemplative life "in the heart of the masses" '. But they have the usual three vows and live in houses with some corporate devotions: this avoids the difficulties but also the possibilities of, say, the original worker-priest experiment. An Anglican attempt with the same general limitations but allowing of a scattered membership still more immersed in ordinary life is the Oratory of the Good Shepherd.[36] This is 'a Society of priests and laymen living under a Rule, which can provide as large an element of common life and discipline as the conditions of work of its members permits'. The group originated among those engaged in theological and pastoral work in Cambridge and at one time had some members living there together who were able even to recite some common offices. It now operates through a number of scattered groups linked by an annual retreat and General Chapter as well as by its rules of prayer and personal finance. But it is solely male and celibate.

There are now more purely 'Protestant' versions of such organizations, the best-known of which is Taizé.[37] But here an important observation must be made. The Taizé community is really a 'Protestantized' version of the Roman tradition of the 'religious' life as it has been applied to communities engaged in outgoing activity (rather than in an enclosed and more contemplative life); this may be seen in the use of the traditional three vows, for example. It is therefore not of much use as an example for those looking for some different type of piety, and it cannot be followed at all by anyone (e.g. the married in an ordinary life-situation) not willing or able to accept these traditional conditions.

All these variations on the traditional themes have the same difficulties for persons in the normal life of the world: they depend on communities (even if only for occasional assembly) and on single-sex, celibate communities at that, even where laity and clergy are both enrolled. They tend to depend, moreover, on vows and on forms of worship and asceticism which may well be open to serious objections (see the last and the next sections) from the point of view of contemporary conditions and consciousness.

Some modern Protestant attempts at a Rule seem potentially at least to avoid some of these difficulties. There is, for example, the Iona Community. As is well known, this community's concern has been the relationship between work and worship, with a special interest in industry and politics. Institutionally, it has centred partly on Iona itself, where members have attended a community week in the summer, and some time was spent there in rebuilding the Abbey. There is also a Community House in Glasgow used for youth and other work. There are about 160 full members (about 30 of them laymen) and a few thousand associates; women can only be associates. The rule of life includes three commitments: devotional (a daily period of prayer and Bible study, though not at a fixed time; and subjects for group intercession); accounting for the use of time; a fixed tithing of income. The rule is implemented by quarterly report cards and an annual renewal of membership.

One further example may be given, that of the East Harlem Protestant parish which was described in Bruce Kenrick's *Come out the Wilderness*. This was an attempt to devise a ministry, religious and social, in the churchless urban wastes, and it illustrates some of the possibilities and problems of group and team ministries generally. For our present purpose it is instructive to notice the difficulties of the group in its corporate devotions and the charge that it became an in-group and exclusive.[38]

It may be suggested, therefore, that in addition to the difficulties noticed above, which come from the traditional

128

conditions which a piety concentrated on God and involving renunciation has seemed to demand, there are difficulties which stem from a confusion of that traditional model with the more 'secular' one implied in following the commandment of devotion to men as primary, and naturally worked out in the world. The sense that devotion to God is also necessary comes out in the attempt to import some weakened version of traditional 'other-worldly' piety, with all the questions this raises of theology and practice.

If, however, a group of people explicitly pursue a piety based on the Second Great Commandment, the problem of rule and discipline, as was pointed out earlier, cannot be evaded altogether. Whether one tries to retain a 'secular' meaning for 'God' 'Christ' and 'Gospel', or simply endeavours to implement some specific standard of conduct, it seems essential to find a means to set up and also to implement a standard of life. In the first case it is particularly important to see that a borrowing from traditional patterns will not do because they reflect a quite different theology as well as a quite different ideal of how the theology is to be lived; and those who in fact are really rejecting the older ideals are going to find the pressures, social and intellectual, which have made difficulties even for those who still try to accept the traditional ways, quite insurmountable for themselves. Those who wish nevertheless to attempt a rule of life will have to realize first of all that this means the acceptance of a common framework of ideas (which for them will certainly not be those underlying traditional rules),[39] an agreed list of areas in which 'commitment' is to be asked for, and a means to inculcate this discipline by some form of what would traditionally have been termed 'spiritual direction'. And all this quite apart from the actual details of how elaborate a rule can be expected from married workers in the world who may meet only rarely.

The third possibility is, we have suggested, the explicit acceptance of the 'traditional' model of devotion to God as primary, involving 'renunciation'; but this to be worked out in the world, and both the model, means and conditions to be explored with a full recognition of the difficulties now involved as they have been discussed so far. What is needed for this is a spirituality both for individuals and also for groups wishing to follow a specifically Christian way of life – for themselves; with each other as Christians; and in the network of 'associational' communities of which they are part by virtue of their homes, work and spare-time interests. The monastery and its derivatives do not help; the traditional patterns of devotion may seem questionable.[40] In this situation it seems necessary to answer two kinds of question. The first is: what kind of spirituality is possible in these conditions? that is to say, what public patterns of worship? what methods of private piety? and, between these, what kind of 'rule of life' linking and stimulating Christians to pursue their ideal, corresponding to the more traditional communities and rules which were mentioned earlier as used for the more traditional pursuit of devotion to God? Without these provisions, it has been contended, we shall tend to lose distinctive Christian standards at all, and indeed leave ourselves and any standards we adopt uncriticized.[41] The other question is: what kind of Church can be and should be expected to emerge if the model of the First Commandment is chosen for Christianity, worked out as a pattern in the world yet involving renunciation and a spiritual discipline? It may well come to be seen that on the model just suggested it is difficult to avoid a picture of the Church as a minority body, indeed a spiritual *élite*. This may seem distasteful: it is certainly in strong contrast – theologically, pastorally and spiritually – with much current reforming activity in the Church.

The remainder of this chapter will be a discussion of the means and methods of a contemporary spirituality which could help to implement the model under the conditions so far suggested; and in doing this we shall have particularly in mind the two types of question just stated.

4. The Methods of Spirituality

(i) Public Patterns

We have seen that the difficulties of public worship involve difficulties about belief in God; the achievement of 'corporateness' in the modern world; the decline in the social ritual functions of corporate religious practice. Attempted answers in terms of 'liturgy' have to face all these problems in an acute form, together with the problem of those who, for various reasons, do not readily approach religious worship in liturgical and particularly in eucharistic terms at all. There is, therefore, unreality at the heart of much liturgical reform in that it does not meet the felt needs of the worshipper, nor do its own symbols always naturally express what they are now intended to symbolize.

Any attempt to cope with this situation must probably face the fact that continuity with the Christian past may have to be reduced to a few basic essentials (e.g. continuity with the aim of concentration on conformity to the will of God in Christ rather than particular liturgical patterns); that a relatively fixed liturgy, even with permitted variations, is too inflexible; that continuing variety in response to varieties of place and time will have to be accepted. Nor should any one norm of type or frequency of services be assumed. In all this what one has to keep clearly in mind are the model of Christianity and the character (intellectual, social, psychological) of the worshipper. The modes of worship are to be adapted to these and not vice versa.

The model, we have said, is absolute devotion to God on

131

the pattern of Christ. If difficulties about belief in God intrude, then they might be tackled by a fresh approach through religious experience in the shape of an approach through the moral impact of Jesus upon the personality on the lines of a Christianized version of Kant's 'categorical imperative'. 'Christianized' because moral experience by itself, though accepted as 'three-fourths of life' in Arnold's phrase, has, if it is to be termed 'Christian' with any meaning, to assume a *specifically* Christ-like shape. The Christian life is to be seen in terms of 'alignment' with this ideal, and worship as the means to achieving this. For example, the Eucharist could be seen in terms of the challenge to contrast one's own life and ideals with those of Jesus and to align oneself with his life, rather than in terms of 'communion' with a 'presence' which would at once involve the ideas of 'God' and 'transcendence' and 'intervention' which cause so much difficulty. 'Alignment' is less subject to these difficulties, for one can be influenced by and committed to an ideal without of necessity raising any further implications. On the other hand, those who are able to live with the more supernaturalist aspects of traditional Christianity are not prevented from doing so. There is, moreover, the possibility of belief and theological reflection on belief in God in a more traditional sense arising out of the actual experience produced by alignment worship – that is, from the effects of moral change in personality. (This may be one meaning of Bonhoeffer's notion of theology renewing itself from a fresh access of religious experience arising out of 'praying and living for others'.)

Some of the problems of recreating worship on these lines are illustrated by the reflections of the Bishop of Woolwich on what he called 'The Aldwych Liturgy'[42] which was in fact simply a secular theatrical performance concerned with the present condition of humanity. Robinson reflected: 'The function of liturgy, as the Church has understood it, is to involve its participants in the saving acts of their redemption. It re-enacts. It overcomes the gulf between what happened two thousand years ago and the believers' life and action in this world now. It is a remembrance of Christ's passion – not in the sense of reminding Christians of past events outside them, but of internalizing and making present those events in and through them. . . .' He admits that the performance was not specifically Christian – 'nevertheless it was a renewal of dedication as the caring community of an intensity that condemns what so often passes for liturgy in our churches'. He concludes that liturgy ought to start like this – 'from the secular crucifixion of our time, in which, as Bonhoeffer said, "Christians stand by God in his hour of grieving" '. Elsewhere[43] Robinson has said the Eucharist should be for men the place 'at which the common and the communal point through to the beyond in their midst', so that 'the vertical of the unconditioned [cuts] into and across the limitations of the merely human fellowship, claiming it for and transforming it into the Body of the living Christ'. This is interesting but perhaps not convincing. Can one indefinitely repeat the (possibly) collective experience of a moment of humanity-centred compassion, and expect this to acquire a specifically Christian moral reference which, moreover, transforms character? Such a project requires more careful preparation and a clearer picture of the kind of moral reaction one is aiming to achieve; and it may even be that mass emotion leads away from and not towards what is desired.

Whether or not this is so, any communal liturgical action should be short, simple and clear, leading to an attempt to confront the worshipper with the contrast between the absolute standards of Christ (in which, ideally, the absolute of God is seen) and the worshipper's actual life. From this should come real conviction of inadequacy, failure, the chastening of the self – its ideals and behaviour – and from this an act of real penitence; and finally a real sense of forgiveness as before God. As has been said, the means by which this is achieved is a secondary matter. It may be suggested that the Eucharist is one means which may symbolically express and help to achieve what has just been described. And such acts of worship ought to provoke, be provoked by, and help to symbolize and continue, the kind of continuing life in the world which we have described as of devotion to God and renunciation within the world.

With this ideal in mind, it may be asked how often such communal acts of worship can usefully be performed. Are they to be extremely frequent, so as to keep up the conscious pressure of alignment and repentance? Or occasional, so as to ensure as far as possible the reality of a repentance liable to be dulled by repetition? How far is such communal repentance really possible? Once again the difficulty of 'community' and in any case of large-scale Christianity comes up. What is the relation between public and private worship on these lines? It may well be that the real basis of spirituality must be in the private piety of the individual, but that both kinds require some middle term of 'spiritual discipline' or 'rule'. To this we now turn.

(ii) 'Community' and 'Rule'

Under this head may be considered such matters as the place and appropriate shape of the Church as an organization; the role of the clergy in it; and the possibility of communities and rules within the wider Church.

The view taken of the *Church* is closely connected both with the view taken of the essential meaning of Christianity, and with the pressures (recognized or not) of modern society. Christians have always differed over the question of whether Christianity is to be regarded as primarily a corporate or an individual relationship with God ('primarily', because the two sides might both be seen as necessary on either view). They have also differed in their estimate of the relationship between the Church as a fellowship of faith and spiritual life with God and men, and the institutions in which this fellowship is embodied: some have regarded these two as virtually indistinguishable or at least inseparable. Then, again, there is the question of the relationship between even the institutionalized Church, and society and its institutions at large.[44] In all this the possibility arises that the condition of society has perpetually conditioned not only the shape but also the ideas of the Church; and even that this is as it should be: it may be that here, as with liturgy, one ought to be prepared to choose between the possibilities just outlined according to the needs of a particular time rather than on the grounds of some allegedly permanent divine plan (for the presence of any such plan ought in any case to be proved, not assumed). For example, it may be that in some periods of history a hierarchical church order firmly embedded in the social order is not only possible but right; whereas in another situation the Church is rightly, as well as necessarily, dissolved into a far looser, even individualistic or at least small group structure. It has been suggested here and there in the earlier parts of this essay that both social and theological considerations may now point to something like this last possibility occurring, whether or not the theorists like it. At the very least the steady decay of the former customary close relationships of Church and society, and the changes in society itself, compel some reappraisal of our views of the Church: it is, we have urged throughout, both necessary and proper to make such factors a part of the material for our theology.

Few people have ventured to posit the destruction of the

Church altogether; it has been more common to attempt to make a Church purely of saints. Such an attempt of course presupposes that some Church is necessary, though it may amount to little more than the convenient association of pious individuals for the reinforcing of their Christian faith and witness. If the Church is viewed in this very practical light it ought logically to be held that the actual form of ministry and organization varies entirely according to the needs of the community – no divine plan is laid down and therefore all is determined by the immediate exigencies of whatever is taken to be the purpose of Christianity. Some such view is implied in John Wesley's organization of Methodism as a doctrinal and practical 'holiness mission'.[45] He relied, however, on a certain link with an existing more traditional Anglican Church, and the later history of Methodism was, as we have seen, one of failure to keep the unity of the body within itself. Wesley also relied on an accepted body of Christian doctrine; and no modern attempt to organize a Church on his basis is likely to have this source of unity. Nevertheless, any radical reformer still confident of a future for organized Church Christianity ought perhaps to consider the virtues of this approach to church order – *if* it could be agreed that order is really secondary and open to choice.

Far more prevalent and, one might say, with the Ecumenical Movement in mind, now dominant, is a view of the Church which implies the necessity of the corporate expression of Christianity and, moreover, in certain necessary forms. There are higher and lower versions of this, but a surprising variety of Christians – high and low, conservative and radical – agree on some such view of the Church as this. The Church is a society which Christ intended and is therefore in the last resort on a supernatural basis and in some sense an indispensable part of God's will which therefore (again, in some sense) cannot fail. There is therefore a visible expression of Christianity in this world which is a comprehensive society of saints and sinners, which really is and must be seen as a society – the Body of Christ – rather than as a human collection of individuals only. The institution has certain divinely-ordained essentials: a separated ministry (which for future Church union must indeed be episcopally organized), sacraments, liturgy. It has a strong, settled, comprehensive institutional basis with which the settled full-time ministry is closely associated. The Church has, so far as possible, some official recognition from society and a recognized place in it, even establishment. Such a Church allows of considerable variety and reform and it is likely enough to represent the general ideals of any future united Church (e.g., in England). It may nevertheless be questioned whether such a Church can produce such an extensive community of varied levels of religious attachment as it did in the past; much less that it can easily incorporate those who take a more sceptical view of the institutional Church as the medium of Christianity. Social considerations by themselves suggest that a Church of this kind will not or even cannot adapt itself sufficiently to changed social conditions (see above, pp.97ff.). By its nature it may in any case attempt to do too much for too many and therefore be committed to too heavy and immobile a structure.

This leaves one more group of possibilities. Perhaps the only common features in this group are the destruction both of the theology and of the institutions of a Church-centred Christianity. One version of this was expressed in what was described as a 'non-church' conference.[46] One of the promoters visualized the future structure of the Church as follows. Negatively, the end of denominationalism, of most church buildings, at least as 'church' buildings, the end of most full-time parsons. Positively, the development of occasional meetings of miscellaneous groups (occurring according to the current structures of society rather than, for instance, by parishes) for miscellaneous purposes of discussion and worship, the latter being thought unlikely to be primary. The overall aim of such gatherings would be to cultivate such a vision of Christian love as they chose, and the participants would not necessarily be Christian in a conventional sense at all. At a subsequent meeting, a reporter suggested that the following sorts of people had attended: those still in the Church but finding it a limitation on their Christianity; those outside, wanting to know Christ and Christian values but not the ordinary Church; and those who wanted to realize something like Christian values, or perhaps some other values, but in any case not necessarily acknowledging Christ. In fact the conference was only able to see itself collectively as one of 'people who ask questions about reality and meaning in human life'.

Two kinds of combined aspiration and disillusionment may therefore be discerned in this evidence. There are those who are as Christians disillusioned with any religious structure likely to emerge from any large-scale united and reformed Church on the lines hinted at earlier. Perhaps the answer for them would be a Church virtually without buildings, full-time clergy or frequent meetings, certainly a Church without the common attempts at providing a church-centred 'social life'. It may well be that parts at least of any Church in the future may have to be organized like this.

There are, however, signs of a more radical disillusionment with anything easily identifiable as Christianity, and once again one sees how much the 'model' of Christianity tends to determine the means sought to satisfy it. The conclusion of the conference did not imply a distinctive *Chris-*

tian faith at all. Yet an unspecific faith may be all that some of our more 'religious' contemporaries can have at present.

It was said above that the 'non-church' idea was one manifestation of a destructive approach to Church-centred Christianity, but that even this breaks down into more or less specifically Christian types. There is, however, another and in some ways even more destructive, yet paradoxically much more specifically Christian, attack on the Church. This was the view of Kierkegaard who saw the Church as an obstacle to Christianity, a way of rebelling against God – 'under the pretext of zeal for God and the things of God to place an abstraction between God and oneself'.[47] The real relationship to God is entirely individual, through an intensely personal and demanding faith. The question, as Kierkegaard saw, is whether by these standards there are ever likely to be enough people to form a Church – even if this is a proper thing to attempt to set up.

No doubt the conservatism of our society will dictate that an attempt is made to continue the institutionalized Church, at any rate in some areas. No doubt also social change and mental change will make it necessary to adopt some of the 'non-church' ideas of a slimmer association which has less plant and personnel and is therefore more adaptable to modern society. No doubt, too, this last is, as an institution, more appropriate than any other to Kierkegaard's and perhaps to Bonhoeffer's vision. Yet it should be clearly recognized that Kierkegaard's vision was for a distinctive Christianity, so distinctive that few could stand it. Anyone taking a view of Christianity as 'renunciation in the world' will have to take this vision seriously and ask himself how far and in what way it is institutionalizable at all. If it is (and certainly there has to be some method of guaranteeing the constant pressure of the vision of God in Christ on the believer's life) then it will be an institution cut down to the bone, for specifically religious purposes only, and centred in the communities in which people are mainly living. Some have seen factories and factory chaplaincies as the appropriate setting – though for social service rather than for worship. But perhaps this is an over-simplification and a misreading of where men's interests really lie.

Turning to the *clergy* as those who traditionally have in most Churches taken a lead in the organization of religious life, some of the points made about church organization are naturally very germane: that is to say, the role of the clergy depends a great deal on the general view taken of the Church. But it also depends on the view taken of the model of the Christian life and how it is to be implemented. At the present moment there is much to suggest a confusion in the ministry about its proper role in the Church and even more in society, and this both for social and theological reasons. The ministry tends to identify itself too easily with the Church; and at the same time worries itself about its declining role in society. Then the attempt is made to solve the problem either by developing more 'church' activities (and so the ministry's own function and control in this narrow setting) or by developing a social role (either Church-based or outside the Church or both) which tends to mean extending the parson's job to cover something else, for example, political and social work. The question then arises, why should he not become a political or social worker – the proper, professional way to do the job? There seems to be more sense in making the parson's job a specifically religious and even theological one, which after all is the area in which, if anywhere, he has some specialized knowledge. But this means accepting the fact that not many are required, and not so much call on his services is likely, nor is he likely to be so much valued by a secularized society: a difficult situation to live with.

Here we may cite some perceptive remarks of Monica Furlong,[48] who suggests that 'the clergyman must live much more in a state of being than in a state of doing'. 'I want them to be people who can by their own happiness and contentment challenge my ideas about status, about success, about money, and so teach me how to live more independently of such drugs. I want them to be people who can dare . . . to refuse to compete with me in strenuousness . . . to read, to sit, to think . . . who have faced the problems of prayer . . . and from whom I can learn some kind of tranquillity.' She recognizes the kind of suffering which all this may involve.

Two possible functions then emerge for the ministry. One is as a kind of perpetual reflection of, or witness to, the reality of God and of a life directed towards God's will in a world which tends to exclude him. The other is to provide such guidance as Christians and would-be Christians can and wish to accept in matters of Christian belief and behaviour. This last raises a number of questions, some of which will be touched on later. For the moment the point should be made that this is not just a matter of 'social case-work'; for what is at stake is religion and not simply social and psychological needs. Further, there is a problem of acceptance on one side and of the nature of 'direction' on the other. Protestants have usually lacked a tradition in this, but it seems necessary for any real repentance and confession in confrontation with Christ to have the guidance or at any rate the presence of someone other than one's self and one's own inadequate self-criticism.

In the fulfilling of these possible roles some minimum organization and discipline is necessary. The ministry at least needs its periods of withdrawal from society for the sustaining of its mental and moral role of testifying to the presence of God and of God's standards; this may be accepted in a way which is impossible and even undesirable for most laymen. How far all ministers are to be full-time would depend on the view taken of the likely size of the future Church and its actual structure, as discussed earlier.

There remains the question of *discipline* for the Church at large, of which the point about 'spiritual direction', as it has just been described, is a part. The question is really how far and in what way in a Christianity defined as following the First Great Commandment, the ideal of 'renunciation' can be cultivated. Some hints have already been given as to the place worship may have in this; and also the place of an 'associational' Church and its ministry. Later we shall look at private piety. Is there something in between these? And for the ordinary lay Christian?

We have already looked at some of the attempts at community and rule and attempted to show their basis and drawbacks. Despite the difficulties there is a case for considering the possible value of these attempts, provided one is clear on what their presuppositions are and how they stand up to modern theological, psychological and social conditions. At the very least it is possible that to uphold the kind of spirituality we have been advocating – a devotion to God which implies 'renunciation', yet within the world – some pattern of symbolic rejection of merely secular and material ideals is necessary. This may require some (?occasional) actual withdrawal from ordinary life in order to clarify and maintain one's basically 'in-worldly' and 'active' life. One way of doing this might be to restrict corporate religious exercises to occasional acts of worship; another might be to reduce 'worship' to an occasional planned 'retreat' of an intense kind. However 'traditional' this may seem to be, the point is that some planned confrontation with the Christian standard is necessary, and one fault in the usual attempts at this has been the dissolution of energy in too many habitual small acts of worship and the consequent reduction of the impact of any more intensive act of 'retreat'. Martin Thornton[49] has actually suggested that a rhythm of 'engagement and withdrawal' which underlies much traditional spirituality could be made the basis for reconciling the demands of a 'radical' theology and traditional spirituality. If one doubts whether he has fully grasped the problems to which radical theology points in its endeavour to cope with secularization, and whether, at the same time, he has fully recognized the difficulties involved in traditionally based religious exercises, the general notion may still not be easily dismissible.

The devising of a pattern of this kind, however, is more easily stated in general terms than actually worked out in practice. The question about detailed means to such a project in fact leads us on to a discussion of some of the main devices for devotion, particularly private devotion, with which the last part of this chapter is to be concerned.

(iii) Private Patterns

Take first the possibility of a modern equivalent of the *ascetic practices* of traditional spirituality.[50] These may be said to have fulfilled two functions: a sign to the self and the world of the 'renunciation' of the world which serious devotion to God entails; and secondly, a means by which such a total devotion to God may be effected in those who accept the ascetic discipline. In traditional spirituality this could only be practised completely through a religious order or some approximation to it: it entailed, that is, a physical separation from the world, or at any rate a denial of some significant part of the world's life. But it may be contended that the means chosen implied not merely that only a minority could hope to achieve real Christianity, but that this minority was cutting itself off from ordinary life at the wrong points – for instance, from family life and daily work. Further, in the present situation it may be contended that the traditional vows at the heart of the ascetic life no longer express effectively even the symbolic face to the world of a life devoted solely to God. Even historically it is not always evident that they have effectively promoted the aim of actually achieving that devotion for those who practised it: celibacy, for example, seems to provoke as many problems as it cures; life in a closed community creates as many tensions as life in the world.

Thus what seems to be required is a set of disciplines – renunciations – which keep the Christian conscious of the tension, rather than the harmony, between God's way and merely secular ways; and which act as such effectively for himself and symbolically for anyone outside. Whether both aims are possible, or should even be sought for, within the same set of acts is certainly an open question. More certain is the fact that the traditional three vows do not readily lend themselves to either purpose. Chastity rules out too many, evades the actual problems of life in the world, certainly does not automatically suggest a reference to God. Nor does obedience in itself. Poverty seems more immediately attractive; yet this, if properly defined (not easy to do in an actual family setting), still does not of itself suggest God. Some measure of public interpretation of the symbol seems necessary, and both the symbol and its interpretation must plausibly suggest God and not merely human protest or compassion.

Two hints at an approach to the double problem of a personal discipline and a witness to the world about God may be found in Kierkegaard and Bonhoeffer. The common factor in their views is the location of the discipline and the witness in the area of 'suffering'. Kierkegaard certainly sometimes wrote as if this should be quite visible and explicit to the world: it was to inculcate and to witness to the 'heterogeneity' (as against the homogeneity) of the Christian with the world. One symbol harked back to the past – celibacy as apparently demanded by the Gospel. But we have seen that this probably lacks in effectiveness and it may well be questioned whether it can be accepted as required by Christ for the very being of a 'perfect' Christian. And Kierkegaard's other thought seems to suggest that Christian suffering is inner and invisible – a constantly recurring inner sense of the contrast between one's ordinary outward life (which includes much that is innocent and perfectly permissible) and the absolute standards and demands of Christ. Out of this comes a continuing moral and religious crisis which is the true Christian suffering, but which also leads to moral and religious progress and is indeed in itself part of that progress.[51]

With this one may, perhaps, compare Bonhoeffer's 'secret discipline'[52] which also involves suffering; but in his case there seems a clearer possibility of the inner suffering necessary for Christian integrity becoming a partial means to open witness to God. He appears to have in mind the description and affirmation of a particular style or attitude of life assumed in the midst of one's this-worldly existence. There is a need for a discipline, a steadfast determination not to belong to the world even as one lives in and for it. Phillips describes the basis of this life as 'Christological' in the sense that one 'shares in the sufferings of God at the hands of a godless world', sufferings hidden in the revealed suffering of Christ. (These last are not therefore merely examples of human suffering: indeed it might be said that disbelief in God, including the Christian's own share in this, are part of contemporary religious suffering.) But this requires not merely Christian participation in secular society; there is also to be true identification and responsibility in the shaping of one's life in tension between being fully in the world and yet deriving one's standards from another kingdom which claims one's ultimate allegiance. And hence the 'apologetic' character of the Christian life – a style of life which points to God. This will be a fragmentary apologetic in this generation, but it does imply a contrast between the world in itself and the world based on a believed yet otherwise inexpressible and intellectually undemonstrable belief in the transcendent or God. It certainly seems difficult to speak of belief in God at all and so of Christianity, unless this notion of a contrast is adhered to.

The centre of much religious devotion in all traditions has been *prayer*. How does this now stand? The fundamental difficulty about prayer in anything like the traditional sense is the same as that in belief in God at all – the problem of finding a 'place' for God and above all for an 'intervening' God. This is sometimes glossed over by reducing the petitionary and intercessory element in prayer to 'spiritual' things; but in fact *all* petition and intercession is up against the same problem of the notion that God actually does anything even to character, for this means ascribing any efficacy in prayer to something other than the praying person and his ideals as held before the mind in prayer.[53] Now this spells the death of much popular religion in much the same way as the decline of belief in what might be called agricultural providence has led to the decline of the hold of worship in its social ritual functions: the 'prayers' of men in despair who do not normally pray at all are not very serious evidence to the contrary.[54] We may associate with this difficulty in traditional prayer the problem of the model chosen for our Christianity: the question here, assuming that prayer is kept, is what kind of spiritual effects are looked for, on what spiritual model and, indeed, by what techniques. Where a secular model of man – and world – regarding religion is followed, the effort and effects of prayer are likely to be in an in-worldly and secular direction. In fact, it is the prayer designed to work actual physical effects which most crudely poses the problem of an intervention which is not really believed in. Consequently, there is all the more pressure to re-define prayer itself, and its objects and methods, in unfamiliar and 'secular' ways. The general aim of this operation often seems still to be an attempt to show that prayer (if properly understood) still 'works'. But this can be done only by substituting for prayer what is in fact either psychological auto-suggestion, or a synonym for practical human action; and this, as in some 'secular' versions of Christianity, really replaces religious belief in God by a human belief in human effort.[55]

This may be illustrated from van Buren[56] who points out that the language of prayer is that of address to someone and we would now find it hard to define who this is; and further that the former use of intercessory prayer for achieving, for instance, agricultural help would now be done by practical action. In this context prayer only makes sense as 'reflection' on the problem in a Christian 'perspective', from which action may follow. This may well be all that can be seen in prayer in the light of the difficulties about belief in God, and, if so, one may recall what was said earlier (pp. 132f.) about Christian faith as 'alignment'. But van Buren's position, it must be recalled, does rule out God as anything but an ideal within humanity, and arbitrarily chooses Jesus as a symbol and with a purely this-worldly reference.

A more conservative view is taken by John Burnaby.[57] Prayer he sees in the light of the New Testament as primarily petitionary – its most embarrassing form – but not working in the crude way which has often been supposed.

God works only through the power of love in men united with his will by the spirit of Jesus. Prayer is an affirmation of this union, not an appeal for a 'miraculous' action of God separated from men's actions. Thus prayer is to align us with God's will, which alters our own situation and the total activity of God in the world. However, we must not expect to see this happening very often, nor necessarily in the way we had visualized. (It may be added that what we shall see happening is most likely to be of the order of moral change, in ourselves and in those directly affected by ourselves.) No one will pretend that this solves all the problems of prayer and of prayer to God as object; but to those able to live with that fundamental belief in God it offers a rational, realistic and moral notion of prayer.

One further and 'radical' challenge to tradition may be cited from Robinson's *Honest to God*.[58] Robinson questions the traditional view of private prayer as in essence a process of *dis*engagement, a turning from the 'world' to 'be with God'; even 'arrow prayers' in the midst of business being really of this type. Traditional schemes of, and aids to prayer have conformed to this pattern, much of the former being in fact adaptations of the monastic hours (a point related to the one we made earlier on attempts at 'rules of life'). Robinson rejects the implication that the distinction between 'holy' and 'secular' is that between a 'religious' area of life and a 'secular' area of life: rather, the whole world should be seen as 'religious' 'in the depth of the common'. Hence 'prayer' should be defined in terms of 'penetration through the world to God rather than of withdrawal from the world to God'. Even if one does have periods of 'withdrawal' these are not to find God – the moment of revelation is more likely to occur in times of involvement and wrestling with actual problems rather than when we are (in the conventional sense) 'praying' about them. Intercession may be understood as opening oneself unconditionally to another in love; seeing him in terms of ultimate concern is to let God into the relationship; and the actual business of giving oneself in this atmosphere is in fact to be in the presence of God and to meet him. The active life of involvement in service thus becomes the life of 'prayer', but Robinson also sees 'special' times of prayer occurring; these, however, occur as a result of pressures arising out of the overspill of a 'prayer'-laden life, and vary in any case according to temperament.

The interesting thing here is the response of the public to this part of *Honest to God*: clearly Robinson's disillusionment with tradition reflected that of other people too (this remains true even if, as some critics thought, he had not fully understood the 'contemplative' tradition). It may be asked, however, whether Robinson has not confused two different things. There is, first, a concern for the world, expressed in action which can only by a misuse of language be called prayer and which can easily cease to be specifically Christian if, as may happen, it becomes an unspecific concern to help people anyway. Second, there is a continuing notion of 'finding God' which is seen in the manner (at least linguistically) of Tillich's 'depth of being'. 'Unconditional love' and 'ultimate concern' are identified with the sense of God and presumably with Christianity – it is doubtful whether this identification can so readily be assumed. Robinson's 'prayer' in fact slides over the problems of belief in God, and of belief in a specifically Christian sense; and furthermore fails to distinguish sufficiently between what we have described as the two basic models of a Christian life – those of the First or Second Commandments. As a result the God-relationship is likely to dissolve in favour of the man-relationship. It may also be suggested that he underestimates the need for a piety which involves, and makes available, self-criticism in the light of a clearer picture of Christ's own specific way.

It seems clear that more attention needs to be paid to *methods of prayer*.[59] Robinson rightly saw that these tend to draw on adaptations of systems designed for men in situations where they can rely on the minimum 'worldly' distractions and also (we may add) on the acceptability and availability of spiritual direction. This is particularly true of the so-called 'Ignatian' method: for this reason alone it is not easy to adapt it to wider use. Further, these traditional patterns of meditation and mental prayer[60] tend to rely either on a 'picturing' of Christ in the Gospel story or on a more verbal apprehension of similar material, applied in each case to individual feelings and needs. All this is subject to some of the general difficulties one is now likely to feel about prayer and is not exempt from some of the peculiar difficulties even of traditional Protestant prayer: that is to say, it has to cope with the loss of an unforced attitude of acceptance of the biblical material – not only of the Psalms (a traditional staple of many schemes) but also of the Gospels. Nor can one omit altogether the difficulties of the supernatural reference: tradition assumes changes of a moral and spiritual kind taking place as a result of the persistent impact of prayer on character, which are due to the 'intervention' of God. In the light of our discussion so far, we have seen that we may well either assume or have to consider the possibility in the back of our minds that it was all a matter of auto-suggestion.

These problems are raised here not to encourage scepticism but to reveal its potential presence and difficulty. Part of the 'suffering' which the Kierkegaardian or Bonhoefferian Christian now has to undergo is mental suffering of an 'intellectual' kind: i.e. the suffering of doubt and scepticism even in his prayers – one aspect of any modern version of the 'dark night of the soul'. Robinson and others really evade the problems of belief in prayer by turning prayer into something humanly easy to understand and do – active help of humanity. The bringing of the 'world' into our piety and vice versa may more effectually be achieved (without losing the attempt at a reference to God) by allowing religious thought, including religious doubt, to be part of any attempt at a contemplation of Christ's character through, for example, the Gospels.

We have already suggested that acts of worship may have to be occasional rather than frequent and habitual – both to conform to the conditions of an in-worldly piety and to keep up the pressure of the ideal against our actual condition; and the same is true, possibly, of private devotion. Intensity over a short period may be the only effective alternative to the monastic continual concentration which for most is frankly impossible without the risk of staleness and self-deception.[61] Whether this is done by an organized retreat, by a purely private enterprise, or by some activity under a spiritual director for the individual, matters less than that the object is to be confronted with Christ intensely with a view to the realignment of character and conduct, the reawakening of a sense of one's life being under scrutiny, one effect being a renewal of the 'renunciation' of conventional social goals – including those of conventional religion. It may well be that to achieve such acts of self-examination some form of spiritual direction is necessary – despite the difficulties already recognized in this. Certainly mere self-cultivation is likely to be self-deceptive.

In all that has been said here to attempt to elucidate the aims and methods of a spirituality which will adequately implement the model of a Christianity based on devotion primarily to God and yet in the world, two final points should be made. One is that, as will be obvious, no final

151

solution has been or can be given to the problems of belief today. Rather, it is contended that these ought to be made explicit and not avoided or excluded from piety either by simply persisting in tradition or in so 'reinterpreting' traditional concepts and practices that they in fact come to be a piety directed to radically different objectives under the guise of the old language: for example, turning devotion to God into devotion to men while retaining the term 'prayer' as if the traditional activity were still being pursued. The other point is that any attempt at the pursuit of God must be an organized and conscious pursuit, but this need not be restricted to any one method even for the individual at all times. For example (a matter which is barely raised here but could well be discussed further) a man may well benefit from the use of a particular method of prayer or a particular book of prayers. George Macleod (followed by Robinson)[62] once referred rather sadly to the 'bankrupt corner' of devotional books used and discarded in a desperate attempt to cultivate a (ministerial) piety. The desperation was not altogether necessary, neither was the feeling of guilt at rejecting a method after a time. No doubt habit and persistence are necessary to use a method to advantage, but it is devotion to God by all and any means which is the real aim; and in our condition of uncertainty and of the dissolution of tradition, it is to be expected that we cannot pray in the same way all our lives. The attempt to do so may well provoke the kind of dryness and lack of critical awareness of our condition which is so dangerous to the whole project.

Conclusion

THE ARGUMENT of this book has been that the present difficulties for a Christian spirituality arise from a complex interaction of factors: the internal pressures and contradictions of different Christian traditions, and the external pressures on belief and life which have been collectively referred to as 'secularization'. The importance of understanding historically and in depth what these factors are is underlined if one accepts the view that religion is not so much an innate as a learnt element in human life. For the same reason one may expect the character of Christian behaviour to change drastically in different periods. It was argued that the fundamental questions to be asked for any spirituality concern the model of Christianity which is presupposed, to which any means must be relatively secondary. The traditional model of the pursuit of God for himself alone, involving some measure of renunciation of the world, had become difficult to follow because of difficulties in belief in God and in the traditional ways of expressing that ideal. The substitution of belief in and service of the neighbour, however, seemed to reduce both the distinctive Christian content of Christianity and its pressure for a standard of distinctive holiness. It was concluded that what was required for a distinctive Christianity was a combination of the traditional devotion to God and a consequent rejection of lesser standards, with a life lived within the framework of normal human existence. The implications of such a project for the character of the Church and its institutions as well as for the specific means to spirituality were then reviewed.

Although the main purpose of this essay has been to lay bare the real issues for spirituality today and to explain the possible alternatives they seem to imply, rather than to lay down a plan of action, some positive conclusions may be ventured. The starting-point for a Christian approach today should be to ask whether or not Christ is accepted as a revelation of God. However difficult such an assumption or act of faith may now seem, most difficult of all to justify or even to express intellectually, no distinctively Christian spirituality can really escape this general position. It may be added that the justification of such a position is likely to grow by experience while continuing to be difficult to express. From this basic position one must consider whether it is possible for real Christianity in our time to be the creed and life of more than a dedicated minority which is prepared to undertake the daunting and painful task of accepting Christ as the point of reference constantly drawing them to the kind of holy life he described.

This Christ-like way of life is marked by an adherence to the First Great Commandment which involves a recurring sense of contrast between the life of the world and of oneself, and that of God as seen in Christ. This leads to a recurring rejection or 'renunciation' of the former and a sense of inadequacy towards the latter, but also to a sense of 'dependence' (as Schleiermacher put it) on God, if only to keep up that necessary challenge to one's own life which is of the essence of holiness and progress in it. From this basic adherence to the First Great Commandment consequences also follow in the area of the Second Great Commandment, but any attempt to reverse this procedure is, we have suggested, less likely to happen. The conditions under which this life is to be lived are those of the ordinary life of participation in the world. The means to this will vary, but are likely to include 'associative' rather than 'communal' patterns of 'church' life, in so far as such a minority Christian existence can go much beyond an individual sense of the pressure of God. Patterns of devotion are to be those of a reasoned and occasional rather than symbolic, ritual, corporate and habitual kind.

In conclusion, it has to be recognized that, if this is the future shape of Christianity, it can never be a popular community religion, and attitudes and reform programmes based on such assumptions have to be rejected in favour of the vision of a minority 'sharing in God's sufferings in the world' – and for the world. Whether this can co-exist with, or live in the midst of, a Christian Church of a more mixed and traditional kind is perhaps one of the more difficult and painful questions to be faced in the immediate future.

CHAPTER 1

[1] *Christian Spirituality*, vol. 1 (Eng. trans. London 1922), preface; see the criticism by Louis Bouyer, *The Spirituality of the New Testament and the Fathers* (Eng. trans. London 1963), preface

[2] *Culture and Anarchy*, ed. J. Dover Wilson (Cambridge 1963), pp. 72ff.

[3] referring to, for example, K. E. Kirk, *The Vision of God* (London 1931); A. R. George, *Communion with God in the New Testament* (London 1953); and a distinction quoted from Deissmann by Gordon Wakefield in *The London Quarterly & Holborn Review*, January 1966, p. 37

[4] This choice is presented to those in the 'evangelical' tradition (and 'discipleship' is preferred) by John Vincent in *Christ and Methodism* (London 1965)

CHAPTER 2

[1] This is pointed out by, for example, Paul E. Johnson, *Psychology of Religion*, rev. ed. (New York 1959), p. 59, citing McDougall. I have drawn on Mr Johnson for some of the psychological points which follow.

[2] apparent, because this is partly a matter of what 'religious' phenomena are in question and in what area. The whole subject, which is involved in the debate about 'secularization', is discussed at a later stage; see also the next note.

[3] see Bryan R. Wilson, *Religion in Secular Society: a Sociological Comment* (London 1966), pp. xv–xvi; and cf. David Martin, 'Towards Eliminating the Concept of Secularization', in Julius Gould (ed.) *Penguin Survey of the Social Sciences* (Harmondsworth 1965), pp. 178f.

[4] Johnson, op. cit., p. 64

[5] This use of 'capacity' is discussed briefly by Ronald Goldman in *Religious Thinking from Childhood to Adolescence* (London 1964), pp. 3–4. He concludes that religion is probably not a separate capacity or any one need or drive, but that it may nevertheless be a 'natural expression of man's basic needs'.

[6] Kierkegaard makes the point in *Philosophical Trifles* (summarized in *Selections from Kierkegaard*, ed. Lee M. Hollander [New York 1960] pp. 17–18) that Socrates had taught that everyone had the truth in him and only needed to be reminded of it. But, says Kierkegaard, suppose that the truth is not innate in man? suppose that he merely has the ability to grasp it when it is presented to him? and suppose the teacher to be of absolute importance – God himself? He concludes that what gives men the impetus to rise into the highest sphere is the consciousness of sin.

[7] Johnson, op. cit., p. 64

[8] Wilson, op. cit., p. xvii

[9] ibid., p. xiii

CHAPTER 3

[1] *Demonstratio Evangelica*, i, 8; quoted from the version in William Law's *Serious Call*, Everyman edition, pp. 95f.

[2] Gregory the Great, *Homilies on Ezechiel*, II, 8; quoted in Christopher Butler, *Western Mysticism* (Grey Arrow edition 1960), p. 223

[3] Gregory the Great, op. cit., II, iv, 6; quoted in Butler, op. cit., p. 235. Butler sees a similar teaching in St Augustine. Both these Fathers, he adds, see

contemplation as open to all; but Augustine 'recognizes that the hermits . . . have unique advantages for the pursuit of contemplation' (p. 221)

4 The theory on which indulgences were based was defined in Pope Clement VI's bull *Unigenitus* (1343); the notorious instructions of Albert of Mainz which helped to provoke Luther's Ninety-five Theses illustrate the situation in the early 16th century: see B. J. Kidd, *Documents illustrative of the Continental Reformation* (Oxford 1911), Nos 1, 6; J. T. MacNeill, *A History of the Cure of Souls* (London 1952), pp. 148ff., 163ff. It is important to note that the indulgence system, though curbed of its abuses later in the 16th century, has never been abandoned and caused a mild flurry at Vatican Council II

5 On the latter phenomenon see, for example, Louis Bouyer, *Life and Liturgy* (Eng. trans. London 1956), Chapter 1

6 J. McManners, *French Ecclesiastical Society under the Ancien Régime* (Manchester 1961)

7 P. Gay, *The Enlightenment: an Interpretation* (London 1967), p. 545

8 Here I follow the analysis of R. R. Palmer, *Catholics and Unbelievers in Eighteenth Century France* (Princeton 1939)

9 The phrase is Gay's, loc. cit.; cf. the same shift in Protestant preaching

10 see *The Last Years: Journals 1853–1855*, ed. and trans. R. Gregor Smith (London 1965) *passim*: especially on Luther and the problem of works and faith (pp. 316–20); and on monasticism (pp. 31, 65–6)

11 Luther, for example, emphasized the necessity of teaching penitence and outward behaviour to ignorant people, mere talk of 'faith' being disastrous (quoted in É. G. Léonard, *A History of Protestantism*, i [London 1966], pp. 117f.). His 'Little Catechism' is an admirable example of such teaching, and Dr Rupp has neatly characterized Luther's alternative to Catholic piety as a 'plain man's pathway to heaven' (see his remarks in *The Old Reformation and the New* [London 1967] Chapter III). For an example of Luther's practical advice on prayer, see *Luther: Letters of Spiritual Counsel*, ed. and trans. T. G. Tappert, Library of Christian Classics 18 (London 1955), pp. 124ff.

12 in his 'Introductory Essay' in *A History of the Methodist Church in Great Britain*, vol. 1 (London 1965), p. xxxvi. But, as we have noticed, the sacramental side of the Reformation had only a limited success.

13 Theirs was a family piety: William Perkins said: 'God's graces may as well be exercised in the family as in the cloister'; it was a piety of plain preaching; and it was aided by catechetical instruction and pastoral care involving a Protestant casuistry: see, for example, H. C. Porter, *Reformation and Reaction in Tudor Cambridge* (Cambridge 1958), Chapter X, from which the Perkins quotation is drawn; and, above all, W. Haller, *The Rise of Puritanism* (New York 1938)

14 The theological tendency of these 'High Churchmen' may be illustrated from the views of, for example, Thorndike on the nature of the Church and the Apostolic Succession, or from Bishop Bull's approximation to the Tridentine doctrine of justification.

15 *Puritan Devotion* (London 1957), pp., 114f. 160–2. It may be noted that English Protestants sometimes felt they lacked an adequate literature of their own on casuistry and therefore drew on Roman manuals (see Thomas Barlow, *Directions for the Choice of Books in the Study of Divinity* [Oxford 1699])

16 Haller, op. cit., discusses the antecedents of this theme.

17 see note 13 above

[18] *Occasional Reflections* (2nd ed. London 1669), p.78; quoted in H. R. McAdoo, *The Spirit of Anglicanism* (London 1965), pp. 270f.

[19] This is discussed in F. E. Stoeffler, *The Rise of Evangelical Pietism* (Leiden 1965), Chapter IV.

[20] for example, in his *Theologische Bedenken*, i, 258–60 (Halle 1701); and M. Schmidt, 'Spener und Luther', in *Luther-Jahrbuch* for 1957

[21] Ritschl in his classic *Geschichte des Pietismus* saw Pietism as a supreme example of the re-introduction of Roman Catholic piety and theology into the Lutheran Church.

[22] This underlines the manner in which the problems involved were universal Protestant problems.

[23] by Gordon Rupp in *A History of the Methodist Church in Great Britain*, loc. cit.

[24] I have given a more detailed justification of the view taken here of Methodism and its contrasts with Evangelical Anglicanism in my *The Future of John Wesley's Methodism* (London 1965)

[25] I owe this point to Dr John Kent; the debt to the Roman tradition in France and the parallel with Fénelon is analysed by Jean Orcibal, 'The Theological Originality of John Wesley and Continental Spirituality', in *A History of the Methodist Church in Great Britain*.

[26] The relations with Methodism are admirably characterized in Dr John Walsh's essay, 'Methodism at the End of the Eighteenth Century', Chapter IX of *A History of the Methodist Church in Great Britain*. It is well known that some early Evangelicals were 'irregular' at least in their early careers, but as fear of secession increased they regretted this.

[27] The standard treatment of the subject is by John C. Bowmer in his *The Sacrament of the Lord's Supper in Early Methodism* (London 1951). Wesley himself was a frequent communicant but his followers could not be in 18th-century conditions; nor did Wesley ever make provision for them to be *frequent* communicants. Consequently, the sacrament could not, in anything like the Roman or later Anglo–Catholic sense, become the centre of piety. An alternative might have been the old Scottish Presbyterian awe of the ordinance heightened by its *occasional* quality and by extensive preparation for it; but I am not aware that early Methodists viewed the matter in quite this way.

[28] 'Protestant spirituality had been in difficulties, however, ever since the moment somewhere in the late sixteenth century when it became evident that the new Gospel . . . was not producing an increase in Christian efficiency . . . Methodism . . . had been the last major Protestant attempt to solve this problem, by bringing holiness . . . down to earth.' It was not a reaction towards Rome but 'a tremendous effort to make a case for Protestant spirituality' – and it failed. (John Kent, 'Problems of a Protestant Spirituality', in *The London Quarterly & Holborn Review*, January 1966, pp. 30f.)

CHAPTER 4

[1] The situation is described primarily in terms of England, since its early industrial development made the processes under discussion more quickly evident; but much that is said here became applicable in due course elsewhere, as will be indicated later.

[2] The double revolution, its interconnexions, and the effects on all aspects of

society including thought and religion have been brilliantly described from a broadly Marxist point of view by E. J. Hobsbawm, *The Age of Revolution: Europe 1789–1848* (London 1962); also illuminating for the general reader on these interconnexions, and less ideological, is D. Thomson, *Europe since Napoleon* (London 1957)

3 The religious census of 1851 is analysed in K. S. Inglis, 'Patterns of Worship in 1851', in *Journal of Ecclesiastical History* (1960), pp. 74–86; see also W. S. F. Pickering, 'The Religious Census of 1851 – a useless experiment?', in *British Journal of Sociology* (1967)

4 That this has been the general trend is here assumed rather than argued in detail, since it is considered that this much at least would be agreed even by those who are sceptical about some of the deductions made from the thesis of secularization.

5 L. Feuerbach, *The Essence of Christianity*, trans. by George Eliot (Harper Torchbook edition 1957), Chapter XII: 'The Omnipotence of Feeling, or the Mystery of Prayer'

6 E. E. Evans-Pritchard, for example, has pointed out, in his *Theories of Primitive Religion* (Oxford 1965), the lack of historical evidence for Freud's religious theories, and he notes further that if God as 'Father' is a sublimated human image, it ought to correspond to the varieties of position held by the father in various societies (pp. 10, 42)

7 see *The Autobiography of Charles Darwin*, ed. N. Barlow (London 1958), pp. 85–96, 235–9

8 For a discussion of some of these points arising out of the wider application of Darwinism, see D. Lack, *Evolutionary Theory and Christian Belief: the Unresolved Conflict* (London 1961)

9 cf. Marx, 'Theses on Feuerbach', in Marx–Engels, *Selected Works*, Eng. trans. (Moscow 1962), ii, 403–5

10 Müller's views are summarized in J. A. Phillips, *The Form of Christ in the World* (London 1967). Müller acknowledges that he goes beyond, rather than merely interprets, Bonhoeffer.

11 D. Thomson, op. cit., pp. 403ff.

12 ibid., p. 862

13 pp. 72–4 below

14 The apparent exception to this in the United States must be noted, but sociologists commonly explain this too in terms of the essentially secular phenomenon of affirming membership in American society.

15 The most perceptive appreciation of the religious outlook of 18th-century England known to the present writer is in A. R. Humphreys, *The Augustan World* (London 1954), Chapter IV, who argues this point of view.

16 This is the significance of Wesley's belief in witchcraft and of his contention that the convulsions of some at least of his converts were evidence of a supernatural struggle which disproved the closed universe of the Deists (*Journal*, standard edition, ed. Curnock, v [London 1914], p. 165).

17 One symptom of the change is the changing attitude to 'adversity' in human life and its religious implications. Thomas a Kempis (*Imitation of Christ*, I, xii: 'Of the Profit of Adversity') sees this as divinely given material for directing men to eternal considerations; modern men see these things neither as inevitable nor as divine, but as conditions to be changed. This may well affect the valuation

put upon traditional asceticism and the forms any contemporary 'renunciation' may take as a spiritual attitude (see later, p. 143f.).

[18] A well-known Roman Catholic charge against Protestantism, which receives a sophisticated restatement in, for example, L. Bouyer, *The Spirit and Forms of Protestantism* (Eng. trans. London 1956) and has some points in common with the approach adopted here.

[19] For a discussion of this, see Chapter 5, section A, below

[20] This point of view is put in E. E. Y. Hales, *Pio Nono* (London 1954) and *The Catholic Church in the Modern World* (London 1958) against more common unsympathetic accounts.

[21] One has in mind the social encyclicals of the Papacy, beginning with Leo XIII's *Rerum Novarum* (1891)

[22] see, for example, F. Boulard, *An Introduction to Religious Sociology* (Eng. transl. London 1960) and A. Dansette, *Destin du catholicisme français 1926–1956* (Paris 1957)

[23] see Dansette, op. cit.; G. Siefer, *The Church and Industrial Society* (London 1960)

[24] Review of Siefer, op. cit., in *New Directions* (Spring 1966), p.42

[25] B. St. John, *The Blessed Virgin in the Nineteenth Century: Apparitions, Revelations, Graces* (London 1903), preface. Mark Pattison (*Memoirs* [London 1885], pp. 211f.) saw Catholics in Paris believing in miracles to the glory of the Church in this way, and compared the attitude of the Newman circle on 'miraculous' punishments to blasphemers; but Evangelicals had a similar tradition.

[26] On 'development', see O. Chadwick, *From Bossuet to Newman: the Idea of Doctrinal Development* (Cambridge 1957); on Modernism, see A. R. Vidler, *The Modernist Movement in the Roman Church: its Origins & Outcome* (Cambridge 1934)

[27] So the encyclical *Pascendi Gregis* (1907) in particular.

[28] as in Loisy's notorious aphorism that what is true for faith may not be true for history.

[29] This seems, for example, to be the case when biblical criticism is accepted. Although its results cast doubt on whether alleged sayings of Jesus are in fact by him, the sayings are nevertheless still authoritative as part of the whole Scripture accepted and authenticated by the Church.

[30] One must nevertheless recognize the fundamental importance of a point made by Professor D. M. MacKinnon on Teilhard de Chardin, that he corrects the tendency of 'radical' theologians to accept the view that 'faith creates its own objects'; Teilhard, on the contrary, sees faith as 'directed towards something outside itself' (article in *Frontier*, Autumn 1965, pp. 169–71).

[31] P. Spencer, *Politics of Belief in Nineteenth-Century France* (London 1954), pp. 91, 93

[32] see L. Bouyer, *Life and Liturgy*; E. B. Koenker, *The Liturgical Renaissance in the Roman Catholic Church* (Chicago 1954)

[33] (London 1967)

[34] see articles in *Frontier* 1967

[35] in *Concilium* (September 1966), p. 53

[36] An exception is 'Does Liturgy make sense?', in *Herder Correspondence*, March 1967.

[37] see Chapter 5, note 35, below

[38] John Kent, 'Problems of a Protestant Spirituality', p. 29

[39] (Dublin 1963)

[40] see also C. Cuénot, 'Spirituality on the Frontier', in *Frontier* (Winter 1966/7), on Teilhard de Chardin's *Le Milieu Divin*

[41] Bryan Wilson's strictures on this (in *Religion in a Secular Society*) as purely anti-quarian, though they include a large measure of truth, do miss this point.

[42] John Kent, 'Protestant Liberalism and the Doctrine of God', in *The London Quarterly & Holborn Review* (July 1964), p. 173

[43] Some illustrations of this are collected in H. G. Wood, *Belief and Unbelief since 1850* (Cambridge 1955), Chapter VI; see also J. S. Bezzant, in *Objections to Christian Belief* (London 1963)

[44] ed. Greene & Hudson (Harper Torchbooks 1960)

[45] ed. cit., Introduction, p. lxxiv

[46] Compare even the young Hegel, who affirmed how much in religion 'injures the dignity of morality, which is independent, spurns any foundation outside itself, and insists on being self-sufficient and self-grounded' ('The Positivity of the Christian Religion', in *On Christianity: Early Theological Writings* [Harper Torchbooks 1961] p. 79).

[47] The phrase is ascribed to Friedrich Schiller by Evans–Pritchard, op. cit., p. 118; the Romantic response is well described in L. Trilling, *Matthew Arnold* (London 1939), pp. 87ff.

[48] F. Schleiermacher, *The Christian Faith* (Eng. trans. Edinburgh 1928), pp. 178ff.; cf. the modern discussion by John Burnaby in *Soundings*, ed. A. R. Vidler (Cambridge 1962), chapter 10

[49] 'In every religion what is sought, with the help of the superhuman spiritual power reverenced by man, is a solution of the contradiction in which man finds himself, as both a part of the world of nature and a spiritual personality claiming to dominate nature. For in the former rôle he is a part of nature, dependent upon her, subject to and confined by other things; but as spirit he is moved by the impulse to maintain his independence against them. In this juncture, religion springs up as faith in superhuman spiritual powers, . . . a match for the pressure of the natural world' (*The Christian Doctrine of Justification and Reconciliation: the Positive Development of the Doctrine* [Eng. trans. 2nd ed. Edinburgh 1902], p. 199).

[50] ibid., p. 205

[51] ibid., pp. 640–6; Ritschl nevertheless allows miracle a place as filling 'gaps' in a causally explained world and so necessary to science's own view of the world (pp. 616f.).

[52] Jean Réville, *Liberal Christianity: its Origin, Nature and Mission* (Eng. trans. London 1903), p. 179 and note; cf. E. Abbott & L. Campbell, *The Life and Letters of Benjamin Jowett*, 2 vols (London 1897), i, 410f.

[53] For some examples, see F. Heiler, *Prayer* (Eng. trans. Oxford 1932), pp. xiiif., and cf. W. Herrmann, *The Communion of the Christian with God* (Eng. trans. 2nd ed. London 1906), p. 230

[54] Herrmann, op. cit., Chapter II. He follows Schleiermacher in seeing that 'we have truly reached God's presence only when, in the very depths of our life, we are conscious of our dependence upon Him. Therefore our communion with God can consist in nothing else than the experience of dependence' (p. 243). The ancestry of some contemporary theologians becomes clear.

[55] Abbott & Campbell, *Life and Letters*, ii, 311ff.; cf. p. 445: 'It is not with the very words of Christ, but with the best form of Christianity as the world has made

it, . . . that we are concerned today. . . . an ideal . . . which may be conveniently spoken of as the life of Christ'; cf., further, ii, 187–9, on a 'modern A Kempis' project.

⁵⁶ see especially *Literature and Dogma* (1873); cf. R. B. Braithwaite, 'An Empiricist's View of the Nature of Religious Belief', (reprinted in I. T. Ramsey [ed.], *Christian Ethics and Contemporary Philosophy* [London 1966]), in which Arnold is cited. For the difficulties in this position, see the discussion in the volume just cited; and on Arnold, see L. Trilling, op. cit.

⁵⁷ He speaks of the 'thoroughly demoralizing' effect of 'making people repeat' certain parts of the Prayer Book. The ideal liturgy would include: '(1) some common feeling concentrated in special acts or words; (2) the greatest latitude for individual thought or prayer; (3) every word should be true; (4) every word should be elevating' (op. cit., i, 435; cf. p. 87).

⁵⁸ 'Everything turns on its being at realities that this worship and its language are aimed. And its anthropomorphic language about God is aimed at a vast, though ill-apprehended reality. So is its materialistic language about the death, the rising again, and the reign of Christ. The language is aimed at a true and inexhaustibly fruitful idea, the idea of death and resurrection as conceived and worked out by Jesus . . .' (Arnold, *God and the Bible*, popular ed. 1903, p. xxviii). But Trilling (op. cit., p. 365) points out the difficulty of using a traditional liturgy with such radical reinterpretations.

⁵⁹ There is an acute analysis of the nature and antecedents of this 'school' in David Pailin, 'Christian and Atheist?', in *The London Quarterly & Holborn Review* (October 1967).

⁶⁰ P. M. van Buren, *The Secular Meaning of the Gospel* (London 1963), pp. 197–8

⁶¹ see R. T. Hardy (ed.), *The Social Gospel in America 1870–1920* (New York 1966)

⁶² Van Buren's description of prayer is discussed below, pp. 147

⁶³ This is discussed below, p. 84, and note 71.

⁶⁴ The phrase is Bonhoeffer's in *Letters and Papers from Prison* (Fontana ed. 1959), p. 92.

⁶⁵ The points made here partly follow the admirable discussion in J. A. Phillips, *The Form of Christ in the World*, pp. 66ff. and Chapter 12.

⁶⁶ *Church Dogmatics*, IV/2, §67

⁶⁷ in his *Concluding Unscientific Postscript* (Eng. trans. Princeton 1941), Book II, part 1; and in *Preparation for a Christian Life*; see also Chapter 2, note 6 above

⁶⁸ *Concluding Unscientific Postscript*, pp. 364f.; cf. *The Last Years: Journals 1853–1855*, passim. This severe standard is applied to 'real' religion in general, not simply to Christianity.

⁶⁹ see the Deer Park picture in *Concluding Unscientific Postscript*, pp. 422ff.

⁷⁰ Here I follow closely the fine analysis of Phillips, op. cit.

⁷¹ cf. *The Cost of Discipleship* (Eng. trans., rev. ed., London 1959) Chap. 1, and Kierkegaard on the 'Absolute'; on a 'space for the Church', see op. cit., pp. 223, 252

⁷² see Phillips on this, and especially Troeltsch, *Protestantism and Progress* (Eng. trans. London 1912), which is more illuminating in the present context than his more famous *Social Teaching*. The references in Bonhoeffer's *Letters and Papers* (pp. 39, 70) to Dilthey are also significant; one suspects that Bonhoeffer's historical sketch of how men have 'come of age' (*Letters and Papers*, p. 122) derives from some such source.

73 An example of this view may be found in H. H. Farmer, *The World and God* (London 1935); and Teilhard de Chardin's speculations, though not of the same type, are essentially immanentist, deriving from the problems and possibilities offered by evolution, and may be felt to be subject to the difficulty mentioned in the text.

74 see note 56 above

75 Humanists and others with a certain 'religious' rather than simply moral view of the world would fit into the picture of this paragraph; consider, for example, the positions suggested by R. W. Hepburn, 'A Critique of Humanist Theology', in H. J. Blackham (ed.), *Objections to Humanism* (London 1963); or the philosophic dedication of Wittgenstein; or perhaps Dag Hammarskjöld's *Markings* – e.g., on the 'road to holiness' (Eng. trans. London 1964, p. 23).

76 For a comment on these lines, see Trilling, op. cit., pp. 56ff. It is common enough in secular histories, as distinct from ecclesiastical histories, of the period.

77 This is evident in Newman, whose final failure to see in Anglicanism signs of the kind of sanctity he regarded as characteristic of the Catholic Church was a crucial factor in his final decision to go to Rome. His *Grammar of Assent*, though written long after his secession, also illustrates the relations of knowledge and faith.

78 The Protestant problem of justification and sanctification in its historic development has been discussed above (Chapter 3). The relations of Evangelicalism with the Oxford Movement were discussed by Yngve Brilioth in his *Three Lectures on Evangelicalism and the Oxford Movement* (London 1934) and *The Anglican Revival* (2nd ed. London 1933), following earlier suggestions that the latter continued the work of the former in another form. A better case might be made for the Tractarians renewing the Wesleyan attempt at a Protestant holiness.

79 see John Kent, 'Problems of a Protestant Spirituality', p. 30, for a parallel between Newman and Kierkegaard on the point of disgust at second-rate Christianity; and on the failure of Anglo-Catholicism, as of Methodism, to achieve its full aims.

80 In any case they believed in the Real Presence, and in ceremonial to honour it, as a matter of revealed theology.

81 J. Clayton, *Father Stanton of St. Alban's, Holborn: a Memoir* (London 1913), pp. 27–8

82 There is a useful collection of material with some dubious attempts at classification of types in D. Voll, *Catholic Evangelicalism* (Eng. trans. London 1963). Voll sees the affair as a borrowing of 'Evangelical' techniques by Anglo-Catholics; but the most distinctively 'Catholic' missioners (for example, Father Benson of Cowley) certainly learnt much from French Catholicism (I owe this point to Dr Kent: see note 84 below).

83 On the late-19th-century Anglican social groups, see, in general, M. B. Reckitt, *Maurice to Temple* (London 1947). Pusey had had a vision of communities of priests in the slums – was this, again, French-inspired? – and Westcott even had a dream of an Order living in poverty with the poor; but what in fact happened was instead the city parson's 'family' of curates or else Anglo-Catholic versions of Catholic religious orders, rather than new ideas.

84 This paragraph and the next deal with topics which have been investigated by Dr Kent in an as yet unpublished study on Revivalism.

[85] John Kent, 'Problems of a Protestant Spirituality', pp. 30–1. For some remarks on the decline of Methodism's brand of spirituality, see G. S. Wakefield, *Methodist Devotion* (London 1966), chaps 2 and 3.

CHAPTER 5

[1] Thomas Luckmann, *Das Problem der Religion in der modernen Gesellschaft* (Freiburg im Breisgau 1963), especially Chapter I

[2] ibid., Chapter III (following, in part, G. H. Mead and Arnold Gehlen)

[3] Helmut Schelsky, 'Ist die Dauerreflektion institutionalisierbar?', in *Zeitschrift für Evangelische Ethik* (1957), pp. 153–74 *passim;* cf. p. 18 above

[4] Harvey Cox, *The Secular City* (London 1965), pp. 20f.

[5] Thomas O'Dea, *The Sociology of Religion* (Englewood Cliffs, N.J. 1966), pp. 80ff.; cf. Luckmann, op. cit., Chapter II

[6] *Religion in a Secular Society*, p. xiv

[7] ibid., p. x; contrast David Martin, 'Towards Eliminating the Concept of Secularization', cited in Chapter 2, note 3 above

[8] It ought to be pointed out that the general 'secularization' hypothesis is not necessarily invalidated by the bad history of some of its sociological exponents. It is remarkable how regularly sociologists repeat the views of Weber on religion and capitalism without showing any awareness of the continuing controversy among historians about their validity. Again, religious anthropologists (e.g., Evans-Pritchard) have warned us about the older exaggerations – indeed, still current – about the non-rational nature of 'primitive' man. The fact remains that change has taken place and that the contrast between the middle ages (or indeed the 17th century) and today is sufficiently clear for the general thesis of secularization to remain reasonable.

[9] 'Towards Eliminating the Concept of Secularization'

[10] Luckmann, op. cit., also recognizes this possibility.

[11] Wilson, op. cit., pp. xv–xvii, argues this too, against Pareto, for example.

[12] Luckmann, op. cit., Chapter II

[13] Wilson, op. cit., p. xi, note 2

[14] For what follows, see Luckmann and Schelsky, *passim*

[15] In this connexion, note the title of Schelsky's article already cited. The whole question of the association of religious *experience* and the forms of *religious observance* is of great importance. Ideally, the two should no doubt coincide completely, but for various reasons there is always likely to be some dissociation. One may surmise that at least for some Christians and other would-be religious people the divergence between what the Churches offer and what the individual feels and believes about religion is now wider than usual. If the attempt is made to align observance with experience a choice has to be made of such experience as can reasonably be regarded as 'Christian', otherwise you you may not get a Christian Church and worship at all. In any case an attempt of this kind is likely to break from or disrupt tradition far more than our usual conservative attempts simply to translate liturgy into 'contemporary' language or shape it in accordance with some ancient 'norm'.

[16] in *Concilium* (September 1966), p. 53.

[17] This language reflects the thinking of Mircea Eliade, *The Sacred and the Profane* (Eng. trans. Harper Torchbook ed. 1961), which is also used by Brian Wicker

in *Culture and Anarchy* (London 1966). On this view, the 'sacred' involves a notion of discontinuity of space and time. In contrast with the modern view of a 'desacralized' world, religious man thinks of the world as being capable, in itself, of revealing a dimension of space and time which is not that of everyday, and this is represented by sacred space (the temple) and sacred time (the festival and myth). Wicker attempts to resolve the problem that men no longer readily recognize a 'space' for God in any sense, by saying that the religious mentality and the reality of the sacred both necessarily involve a community sense. 'Thus, for Christianity, the sacred space is not that of the consecrated building, but rather the space which is created by the presence of the members of the community to each other' (*Culture and Anarchy*, p. 218). On this basis one can recover the sense of God, Church and liturgy. This is a satisfyingly 'Catholic' way to be modern – Wicker prefers 'radical' – and traditional at the same time; but one may question whether it does justice to sociological realities or to the problems of belief, any more than Geffré's rather similar conclusion in the text above. The assumption of an in-bred sense of community does not logically or existentially require a belief in God; and a lack of this sense does not imply a lack of belief, but does imply a different expression of it from the one that Wicker, and Geffré, wish to implement.

18 cf. the views of Acquaviva (as cited by Wilson, op. cit., p. xv note), who thinks a sense of holiness is communicated by myth and symbol; holiness has declined but symbol has persisted, and the process is not necessarily irreversible. This is perhaps questionable (see p. 121 below, on the problems of symbolism in relation to the Liturgical Movement).

19 see note 17 above

20 Harvey Cox (op. cit., pp. 20f.) usefully distinguishes between 'secularization', which he sees as essentially a liberating force for religion, and 'secularism' as an ideology, a new closed world-view which functions like a new religion and is as dangerous to the 'openness' of secularization as it is to religion.

21 John Kent, 'Problems of a Protestant Spirituality', p. 32

22 Kent, op. cit., and in personal conversation

23 Acknowledgement as in note 22

24 L. Bouyer, *Life and Liturgy*, p. 1, and Chapter I *passim*

25 So, for example, Brian Wicker, *Culture and Anarchy*

26 John Kent, 'The Psychology of Worship', in *The London Quarterly & Holborn Review* (January 1964), p. 53; on which what immediately follows is based.

27 On the history and principles of the Liturgical Movement, see J. H. Srawley, *The Liturgical Movement: its Origin and Growth* (London 1954); A. R. Shands, *The Liturgical Movement and the Local Church* (London 1959); and especially E. B. Koenker, *The Liturgical Renaissance in the Roman Catholic Church*

28 Harvey Cox, op. cit., makes some sensible comments on this, as against the attitude of some sociologists deploring urbanism; though there are many dubious arguments and some strained biblical exegesis in his book.

29 The argument which follows is succinctly put by Kent in 'The Psychology of Worship'.

30 Although it is absurd to bring in such a large subject in a mere footnote, it may be as well to refer here to the interesting work of Paul Verghese, *The Joy of Freedom: Eastern Worship and Modern Man* (London 1967), especially Chapter I, which makes some good points about the difficulties of a contemporary

spirituality. Yet it may be doubted whether the Eastern tradition can for ever escape the secular tensions of the West; whether, in any case, the Eastern way can very easily be absorbed even by a devout and conservative Western Christian; and whether, above all, one can solve the underlying problems of any modern spirituality simply by trying to fall back on yet another tradition which depends on radically other presuppositions than those which control the present day.

[31] as in, for example, the works of Bouyer or Wicker already cited

[32] see the strong suggestion of this in Luther at least, in the *Babylonian Captivity of the Church*, and compare the rubric at the end of the Book of Common Prayer service for Communion of the Sick which admits of full sacramental benefits to the faith of a sick man who, in an emergency, cannot receive the elements.

[33] Wilson, op. cit., p. xviii; and compare his comments on the function of the Ecumenical and Liturgical Movements as a means for providing a function for the clergy: points which should not be dismissed out of hand, even if this is an incomplete explanation.

[34] For some of the difficulties of the traditional religious orders and their practice of prayer, especially in relation to contemplation and the use of Scripture, see G. Every, 'The Decay of Monastic Vision', in *Theoria to Theory*, vol. i (October 1966)

[35] For some description of them, see G. Siefer, *The Church and Industrial Society*, pp. 88ff. and references

[36] For details, see P. F. Anson, *The Call of the Cloister* (rev. ed. London 1958), pp. 181ff.

[37] see *The Rule of Taizé* (Taizé 1965), set out in both French and English

[38] Bruce Kenrick, *Come out the Wilderness* (Fontana ed. 1965), especially Chapters 17, 20

[39] For example, prayer in the traditional sense becomes difficult if God is not really the object of devotion (see pp. 147 below, on van Buren's idea of prayer). Rules of social conduct are more relevant in this setting of belief; but in what sense can these be set in reference to Christ if Christ is seen humanistically?

[40] Where the problem is 'a spirituality of the housing estate', monasticism 'is less help than the psychiatric workers and sociologists and others who are analysing the nature of small groups, the meaning of group therapy, and so on' (Kent, 'Problems of a Protestant Spirituality', p. 28).

[41] cf. Matthew Arnold, who wrote (in the poem 'Morality'): 'tasks in hours of insight will'd Can be through hours of gloom fulfill'd.' Jowett was similar in his desire to see prayer as moral meditation concentrated on God and the ideal with a view to improving the self (Abbott & Campbell, op. cit., i, 410f.), which for him, when tired of chapel prayers, rose to the pitch of a daily return to thoughts 'of death and of God, and of the improvement of human nature' (ibid., ii, 190).

[42] An article in the *Guardian* (date not now known)

[43] *Honest to God* (London 1963), p. 88f. He recognizes that it often fails to be this.

[44] Of the enormous literature on the theology of 'the Church', the two books which raise the more radical questions most usefully, in the present writer's view, are E. Brunner, *The Misunderstanding of the Church* (Eng. trans. London

1952) and Eduard Schweizer, *Church Order in the New Testament* (Eng. trans. London 1961).

45 I have given a short treatment of Wesley from this point of view in Chapter I of my *The Future of John Wesley's Methodism*.

46 see the articles by Ray Billington in *Methodist Recorder* (April 1966) and *New Christian* (2 June 1966); and the report of a 'non-church conference' in *New Christian* (12 January 1967)

47 *The Last Years: Journals 1853–1855*, p. 297. He adds: 'Men have struck on the idea of turning it [the Church] into a person, and by first speaking spiritually about it as a person, about its birth and the course of its life, and so on, in the end grow accustomed to identifying the church with Christians – and there are no Christians in any other sense than this.'

48 'The Parson's Role Today', in *New Christian* (16 June 1966)

49 *The Rock and the River* (London 1965)

50 Some of these points I owe to an unpublished paper by John Kent.

51 see his *Concluding Unscientific Postscript*, pp. 446f.

52 see *Letters and Papers from Prison, passim;* J. A. Phillips, *The Form of Christ in the World*, pp. 225ff.

53 Compare Jowett's problems (references in note 41 above).

54 This point is well made by D. Z. Phillips, *The Concept of Prayer* (London 1965), pp. 115f.

55 The logical problems involved in the concept of prayer are examined by D. Z. Phillips, op. cit.

56 Van Buren, *The Secular Meaning of the Gospel*, pp. 188–90

57 in *Soundings*, Chapter 10

58 *Honest to God*, Chapter 5; *The Honest to God Debate* (London 1963), pp. 66, 79, 85

59 This paragraph, again, is indebted to some remarks of John Kent.

60 see, for example, the tradition of Lancelot Andrewes's *Preces Privatae* or the *Cuddesdon Office Book* as examples of private and public patterns of ordered devotion; and Wilfred L. Knox's *Meditation and Mental Prayer* (London 1958), which is an example of an attempt to offer 'mental prayer' for everyman's use.

61 despite Knox, and the persistent plea in, for example, Butler's *Western Mysticism*. The celebrated example of Brother Lawrence's *Practice of the Presence of God* tends to illustrate the risk of perpetuating a particular state of feeling which really rules out fresh insight into one's condition: a risk to which those early Methodists who claimed to have an 'experience' of perfection or pure love were also prone.

62 George Macleod, *Only One Way Left* (Iona Community 1956), pp. 100f.

Index

Index